WHEN ALL
ELSE FAILS

To Valerie,
God Bless you!
& Happy Reading

Donna M Young

WHEN ALL ELSE FAILS

DONNA M. YOUNG

Published by Donna M. Young
P O Box 76, Lawton, IA 51030
dmywriting@wiatel.net

Author photo by Elizabeth Rose Kahl

Published in the United States of America
ISBN: 978-1-947143-02-9
Biography & Autobiography / Religious

ACKNOWLEDGMENTS

My utmost gratitude will always be for my sweet Lord Jesus. Thank you for giving me the words to say and a desire to share the joy and hope with which you've so generously filled my heart.

Throughout this cancer journey, I have been surrounded by family and friends who've helped me, cared for me, prayed for me, and encouraged me in so many ways. I don't know what I would have done without their strength and support. Thank you first to my family: my husband Marty; my children and their significant others, Aaron, Alicia, Elizabeth, and George; Jarrod and Stephanie; David and Kara; sisters Robin Loving and Bobbi Kelly and brother Richard Quiggle; father- and mother-in-law Vern and Mary Graham; brother-in-law Jim

Young, his wife Ronda and sweet Rachel; my Aunt Barbara Greene, Uncle Floyd Ellison, Uncle Allen Ellison and Aunt Chris, and my Aunt Lynette Wyatt; cousins Barbara Anne Greene and Dianna Fellner; grandchildren Kirra, Varek, Annika, Trinity, and Elijah. And my friends Barb Hinrickson; Bill and Amy Prato; Caleb and Emily Widman; Dave, Katherine, Audrey and Megan Hanson; Donna Gardner; my general practitioner Lori Krause; Leslie Riediger; Lorna Peters; Maryanne Zenor; Mike and Renee Anson family; Pat Washburn; Pat Watkins; Tom and Judy Rich.

Many local pastors and churches have also held me up in prayer and even volunteered their time and members to help with the organization and execution of a cancer benefit in my honor. I would like to sincerely thank any and all who have had a part in serving, whether financially, through prayer, through action, or encouragement. Some of those names follow in alphabetical order. I hope to not leave anyone out, but I am human, so I extend a heartfelt thank you to anyone who has reached out to me, or held me up in any way. God bless you all.

Thank you to Bethel Lutheran Church and Pastor Bruce Jackson; Climbing Hill Baptist Church and Pastor Roy and Phyllis Struble; First Christian Church and sister Emily Frady and sister Deanne Hanson; First Congregational United Church of Christ and Pastor Al and Alaire Willits; Glendale Baptist Church and Pastor Jim and Sharol Wilson; Kingsley United Church of Christ and Pastor Bob Blair; Lawton Community Presbyterian Church and Pastor Cindy Ripperger; LeMars Bible Church and Pastor Fred Gums; Morningside Bible Church and pastor Terry Emke; Open Door Bible Church and Pastors Mike and Judy Smith; Word of Life Church and Pastor Wally and Jane Greene.

I would also like to extend a huge thank you to all the doctors, nurses, nurses' aides, techs, study specialists, administrative assistants, and others at the June E. Nylen Cancer Center and Unity Point St. Luke's Hospital who have been so kind and helpful, with a special thanks to Mary Jane Fitch, for getting things started; Dr. Luis Lebredo, Dr. Hagen, Dr. Wender, and Dr. Smith; Cindy Gates, for always having a kind word and a hug; Brenda

Winkler, for going to bat for me, Sister Janet and especially, Shari Black, the best in her field, who always listens and follows through. I love you all, God bless you.

CONTENTS

INTRODUCTION

Over the past few years, I discovered I had a problem; quite a serious one really for someone who claims to be a Christian. One that was keeping me from living the fulfilled, confident life in Christ, which He died and rose again for me to live. I began to wonder if there were others, maybe even other Christians, who were suffering from the same dilemma.

The problem which plagued me could be boiled down to an often used term, "When all else fails." I used that expression in passing on an almost daily basis, but didn't realize how flippant it sounded until my very life depended on it. All my adulthood, even as a pastor's wife, I'd used that term. By it, I meant in essence: when we've done every single thing we can do, thrown all our own resources at it, we can finally give in, break down, and resort to prayer. After all, we should try to solve everything ourselves before bothering God with it, shouldn't we? He's so busy with all the really important stuff (that is if He's even listening), and maybe in the larger scheme of things, my troubles aren't such a big deal to Him, are they? I didn't have a problem believing there is a God sitting on a throne somewhere in heaven, I guess; or even that He might answer prayers for all those really good, deserving people who know how to pray. I just had a really hard time believing He would bother to spend His time and resources on someone as worthless and insignificant as me. I hadn't grown up praying much, and until I married my husband, no one ever really tried to teach me how to pray. But even after I'd learned the basics of how to pray, it still seemed to be my last resort especially in serious circumstances. Those situations usually sent me first into a panic and then into confusion as I tried to create my own solutions.

I hadn't yet come to see the grace available to me by trusting Jesus and the value of going to God in earnest prayer.

I have to admit that, as a pastor's wife, I got pretty good at the fancy, frilly, wordy prayers for a few of those years; the ones that when I look back, I believe must have made me look to God like the Pharisee who prayed next to the tax collector in Luke 18:10–14. I'd actually been told before by folks in our church congregations that I gave great prayers (I was very proud of this), so I really went to town on that one. I think deep down inside I felt the more elaborate the prayer and the more holy my voice sounded, the more likely I was to catch God's attention; but did I believe He would actually answer those prayers? Well, not for me. I hadn't learned yet, by that point in time, how to completely lean on Jesus as my source; and sadly we, as pastors and leaders, weren't teaching our congregation how to depend 100 percent on him either.

When people were hungry and thirsty, we did what James told us to do in chapter 2; we fed and clothed and found this portion of our Christian duty fairly easy to achieve.

> What good is it, my brothers, if someone says he has faith but does not have works? Can faith save him? If a brother or sister is poorly clothed and lacking in daily food, and one of you says to them, "Go in peace, be warmed and filled," without giving them the things needed for the body, what good is that? So also faith by itself, if it does not have works, is dead. (James 2:14–17, ESV)

We bought them groceries, as we should have, but we weren't helping them learn how to drink from a well that never runs dry. Instead they were depending on us for sustenance. If anyone decided they didn't have the resources to pay a bill, we paid it for them even when it put us in a desperate place financially.

We told people in our congregation to trust Jesus; that God loved them and wanted them to be prosperous. But, when one was about to be evicted from her apartment, or his automobile was about to be repossessed and they came to us with fists raised saying, "You told me God would take care of me," we didn't teach them how to pray and be dependent on God for their answers and supply; over and over again, we simply took money from our checking, then our savings, then our 401ks and finally put their problems on our credit cards to prove to them we hadn't lied about His love, and that God really did care about them after all.

How could we expect those who followed us to believe for themselves when we didn't truly believe in, or live out, His infinite unquestionable power either—as we proved by example every day—and instead took the easy way out? God didn't want us spending money we didn't have in order to make people trust Him. He didn't need our help in that department or any other. Without realizing it at the time, we were replacing God with a credit card and not giving Him the time or opportunity to act without our interference. Our finances became so overwhelmed we caused ourselves to be insolvent. Once we ran out of money, a number of people stopped coming to our church. We searched them out, but they continued to avoid us. After all, when you are only following the loaves and fishes, don't you leave when the basket is empty?

I don't think, before the events of these past five years, I'd ever really thought of prayer as the first essential step in any process, but only something to use after the last desperate attempts to try to fix my own circumstances had collapsed around my clay feet; a last chance to beg for help from a source I didn't really trust anyway.

Prayers like these were common: Lord, if you'll help me this once; if you'll just get me out of this mess; if you'll save me I promise I will…. The problem with begging for God's help, instead of believing on His already provided grace, is that we tend to make promises we can't keep. When we don't keep our promises, we believe God is mad at us; we allow guilt to overwhelm us, and that takes us farther away from the only one who can truly help us through answered prayer.

When I began, very slowly at first, to realize how much Jesus loves me, and that He is a very present help in times of trouble; a real, current, loving God who already died and rose again to cure our troubles and fulfill all our needs two thousand years before we were ever born, I finally stood in awe of His power to heal me, to deliver me, to empower me, and to fill me with all the grace I will ever need to overcome any situation—to be a victor in any battle—and prayer at last became my first, and eventually, my only line of defense!

I have come to understand through many trials that Satan's job is to convince us God doesn't care or have time to deal with our problems. If he can cause us to doubt God's intentions toward us or His unconditional love for us, he has done his wicked job very well. Sadly, in my life, I allowed Satan's voice to overwhelm the voice of Jesus over and over again for many years. I lived in doubt instead of faith.

Jesus says it best when he explains to us in John 10:10 that the thief, Satan, comes only to destroy!

> The thief comes only to steal and kill and destroy. I came that they may have life and have it abundantly. (John 10:10, ESV)

It was essential then that I would learn to live in faith instead of doubt!

But let him ask in faith, with no doubting, for he who doubts is like a wave of the sea driven and tossed by the wind. (James 1:6, esv)

I praise God that He stuck it out with me even when, if I were Him, I probably would have given up on me and thrown in the towel long ago; I thank Him for the magnificent way He has moved in my life to bring me closer to the knowledge of His unconditional love and grace. And I thank Him for that most powerful tool He has given us—the power of prayer.

What follows is a small piece of my journey.

The Attack

November 4, 2010.

"I'm really sorry to have to tell you this, Mrs. Young, but the cancer has spread," the oncologist at the cancer center announced in his consoling, yet professional tone. That certainly wasn't what I'd expected to hear, and my ability to receive new information shut down tight for a moment. I closed my eyes and composed myself before looking back up. His gaze was compassionate, but not in the slightest bit hopeful. Shaking my head, I stared up disbelieving into his otherwise seemingly competent face, searching for any sign of possible mistaken identity.

"If you'll look at the report, here, it explains everything in detail and lists the six locations of current metastases," and then he began to verbally list those locations replete with medical terms and other intelligent gibberish I couldn't understand in my currently dazed state. When he was finished, he held the report out to me as if he wanted me to take it. I didn't want it. I felt as if by touching the paper it might somehow indicate my agreement with this impossible diagnosis. I glanced around the room frantically, looking, as it were, for a means of escape, but saw none.

"Okay," I finally answered softly. "What stage is it and what kinds of options do I have? I really don't know what I'm supposed to do. I guess I thought the double mastectomy was supposed to remove the tumors and the effected tissue?"

"Well, of course, that was the objective of the initial procedure," he explained, "but when you came to us, as it clearly shows on the PET scans, the disease had already metastasized and extended far beyond the originally involved sites. It would have been unreasonable to expect that the surgeon could have known that without seeing the scans, which, as you know, were only done later. He would have been dealing with what was originally located through the biopsies and trying to contain the known situation as much as possible. With so many lymph nodes engaged, it isn't a surprise to find stage four results. I'll let the three of you talk. If you need me, you can ask the nurse and she will reach me." With that, the doctor left the room.

Stage four, I thought. *Oh my god, doesn't that mean terminal?* When I finally read the report later at home, my eyes were drawn immediately to the section which read, "Incurable, stage four…"

My husband, who is also my pastor; and our son, a newly graduated Marine, sat stunned. I felt as if someone had punched me in the gut. I couldn't breathe normally. Mind racing with all the questions I should have asked, but didn't know how to approach; I'd been too surprised by his kindly but blunt words to form coherent thoughts. I would soon have the opportunity to ask those questions and find out how serious my prognosis truly was. For now, I knew it was a priority for me to stay in control of my emotions and try to show calm to my family.

A little more than two months before that November 4 pronouncement, we—my husband Marty, our daughter Liz, and I—prepared to leave for San Diego, California. We were on our way to witness our son David's graduation from Marine boot camp at Pendleton. Scrimping and saving all summer, Marty took on extra painting jobs (as you might know, most pastors don't make much money) to come up with funds for the trip; we intended to make this time as close to a family vacation as we'd had in a good many years. We each took two weeks off work, excited about our time away.

David had no certain knowledge that we'd even be able to attend his graduation since we had no contact with him except through the US postal service. And on last contact, we'd told him we weren't sure we could come up with enough cash for the journey, so we were anxious to surprise him and enjoy some much needed and happily anticipated R & R.

I'd been exercising like a fiend trying to lose a little weight (all those potlucks over the years had taken a toll) and get in shape for our upcoming jaunt, to no avail, but I didn't give up. Losing weight for me has always been a bit of an uphill battle, and I'd been rising before dawn each day for many months to walk three miles and do a half hour of calisthenics and weight training. I would continue that regimen on our journey, wondering all the while why I felt more exhausted with each passing day. Perhaps it was the time change? We do live in Iowa, so there was a two-hour difference between Central time and Pacific to consider.

We left home on a beautiful September day, before the crack of dawn, to begin our trip. The air was crisp and cool, and I could feel the coming of fall in the air, my favorite season. We were full of the enthusiasm and eagerness you would expect for a momentous occasion such as the one we were about to experience.

We had a great time in San Diego. David's platoon scored highest in his battalion during their time in training, and they were recognized during graduation ceremony in the sweltering California heat. Dave looked handsome in his uniform, and we were all very proud of his accomplishments. Allowed to take a few days off base with us before he would fly home for leave, we were able to investigate the local sights to our heart's content. He'd be going back to Pendleton after some leave time to begin his combat training before MOS school and later, deployment to Afghanistan and the desert heat.

Back at home, I was even more exhausted than before, but figured it was the result of our travels and ignored that as well. After all, we were getting older, six children and, at that time, nineteen grandchildren between us, and things had certainly been busy.

Dave left for San Diego at daybreak on Friday, the first of October. We would miss him. It'd been great to have him home for awhile, but we all had to return to work on the following Monday, and there was still lots to do to prepare, so I spent the weekend getting things ready.

I mentioned before that my husband is also our pastor, but he'd recently left the church he'd served for a number of years and was instead helping with the preaching and music at the Gospel Mission in town and doing pulpit supply for several churches in our area while he did light carpentry, painting, and drywall work, in order to pay bills.

Dave worked with him until he joined the Marines, and on occasion, our daughter Liz helped out for a few days at a time, though at that time, her full-time job was counseling for at-risk youth at a local recovery center. I was working as secretary and office manager of a large church in Sioux City, but I can certainly remember scraping a bit of paint myself; and we stayed active in our community, with our kids and grandchildren and with the goings-on of regular day-to-day living, so it wasn't surprising that I'd been stressed enough to miss it.

On Monday, the fourth of October, I woke to go for my daily walk, and as I stretched, I felt a sharp pain in my left breast. My hand moved instinctively to the twinge, and as I touched the area, I gasped out loud. Marty, still mostly asleep asked, "What's the matter?"

"Nothing, honey, going for my walk now, I'll wake you when I get back."

"Okay, love you," he mumbled.

I didn't need anyone to tell me what the large egg-shaped lump in my breast was. It was solid and fixed, and though I'd already guessed, I didn't want to worry anyone else, so I wasn't about to tell my family anything until I was sure I had a handle on the situation.

When I arrived at work that Monday, I wasn't entirely sure what to do, but I knew I had lots of work to catch up on and a monthly newsletter to get out for the congregation, so I put off the inevitable until I had a few items finished and some time to myself.

We'd always been healthy, and my husband was a self-employed pastor, so by default we had no health insurance. I hadn't been to a doctor in years, and I wasn't sure who to call. On my break, I looked through the phone book and noticed a listing for the cancer center. I called. Telling the receptionist my suspicions and that I didn't have a family doctor, she put me through to a kind woman who was the cancer center's patient advocate at that time. Mary Jane Fitch was her name. One of the kindest human beings I've ever had the pleasure to know, though she has since retired and I don't see much of her anymore, she was gracious and infinitely helpful. I was grateful she was there to help me when I needed her. She was wonderfully warm and believed unflinchingly in a woman's intuition. I thank God for her and for her help.

UNCERTAINTY

The next few days were a bit of a blur. My advocate arranged for me to see a doctor on Tuesday, but I asked her to change the appointment for Wednesday so I could finish my newsletter and get my work up-to-date. I believe I knew instinctively that once I walked into the doctor's office, I wouldn't be back for quite some time, and I didn't want to leave the church where I was happily employed in a state of confusion and disarray.

On Wednesday, all caught up at work, and with various instructions posted on lists in the office, I left for my appointment. Somewhere in the back of my mind, I still hoped this was all a terrible mistake and that the physician would tell me my only problem was that I had a vivid imagination. I just wanted to hear, "All is well," from someone in the know.

In the doctor's office, I donned the customary gown and waited for the physician and his nurse to arrive. Millions of thoughts sped through my mind. One of the strangest was the deep longing for my mom to be there with me. It was a bizarre thought for many reasons. One of them being she'd been gone for almost twenty-five years at that time, and another was that she'd died of alcohol-related causes and had never fully "been there" for me in my life, so it was difficult to understand why I would desire her comfort so desperately now.

When the doc entered the room, he introduced himself as his nurse helped me onto the exam table. He began in a bit of a condescending tone to ask me, "Can you tell me why we are examining you today?"

"Yes," I replied, "I believe I have breast cancer."

"Can I ask who has diagnosed you with breast cancer?" he said, with a sneer.

"Well, no one has diagnosed me yet. It's just a feeling I have."

"Well, let's see if we can get you looked over and out of here so you can stop your worrying, okay?"

He began examining my right breast all the while giving his nurse a knowing look across the table. I could tell he believed me to be just another hysterical middle-aged woman and felt I was wasting his time. I started to second guess myself and felt embarrassed to be taking up his valuable time. When he moved to my left breast, he began on the inner quadrant and slowly moved to the outside all the while exchanging looks with his assistant.

As his hand moved to where I'd felt the lump, I watched his eyes grow big as saucers and he asked his nurse for a tool. He began measuring, and she began writing. He told me they would be right back and went to the hall outside the exam room. I don't know if they didn't realize he hadn't fully closed the door, or if at this point, it just didn't matter. The doctor spoke in urgent tones to his helper and gave her a list of tasks to accomplish. When they came back in the room, he told me they'd arranged an appointment for me at the Breast Clinic in Dakota Dunes and wanted to know if I had someone who could go with me since it was urgent that I go right now. Okay, so it was finally time to call in reinforcements.

My husband rushed over, upset that I hadn't told him what was going on, and drove me to my visit. An attempt at a mammogram yielded strange results. The lump was so large and ungainly the technician couldn't get a true reading on its size, but the unanimous consensus was this bulge needed further investigation.

Informing me that the next day, Thursday, would normally be her day off, the doctor and her assistant were both agreeable to coming in and doing an ultrasound and biopsy if I was also willing. I decided that would be a terrific idea and thanked her for her generosity.

I worried myself half to death that night and got very little sleep, waking early to go for an extra long walk. On my walk, I cried and begged. I would love to be able to tell you that, as a pastor's wife, I wasn't concerned. That my faith was strong and I completely trusted the Lord, but I would be lying to you. I didn't trust anyone back in those days, least of all God. I'd also love to tell you that my husband, who is a pastor, wasn't concerned and knew that God had everything under control, but that would also be a lie. Marty and I drove to my appointment in silence. I was frightened beyond words, and he didn't have a clue as to what to say to comfort me through this trial.

It's kind of strange, looking back, that I wasn't already completely confident in the Lord, for a number of reasons. I'd actually been healed before. A young girl in our congregation laid hands on me during a special healing service at our church, and I was miraculously healed of scar tissue on my back—scar tissue caused by a car accident, which had given me severe pain in my left, lower back for years—but I'd figured God used that circumstance to get others to come forward as some had even given their lives to Jesus that night; and perhaps as a way to encourage the young girl who'd laid hands on me. I guess I reasoned I was just the lucky recipient of the overflow.

I'd also been healed of severe hearing loss. A condition I'd suffered most of my life due to abuse and relentless childhood ear infections; when my husband, hearing the voice of God in his spirit, came up behind me and stuck his fingers in my ears. I know that sounds strange, but Marty follows the leading of the Holy Spirit, and I'm glad he did, as my hearing went from 40 percent loss in my left ear and 60 percent loss in my right to perfect hearing in both ears! I knew though that God had healed me on that occasion because my husband was faithful. Marty deserved a miracle, I rationalized, and it certainly wasn't because of me.

Our daughter Liz had also been healed of a possibly deadly condition after we had prayed over her and anointed her with oil, but of course my beautiful daughter would deserve God's healing. That was a no-brainer.

Marty too had been healed of very painful sinus infections, which had plagued him for decades and was now pain free for several years, so why did I doubt? I doubted because I didn't understand God's grace. I still thought it had something to do with me. I still thought I had to do good things all the time, to deserve good things from God and I knew, due to my own life's mess, I didn't merit anything good from anyone.

Chilly on the Thursday morning of my scheduled biopsy, I left my jeans and socks on while I swathed my upper body in a clean, flowered gown and climbed on to the cold, metal exam table in the center's ultrasound room. The nurse covered me with a warm blanket and pulled out a sophisticated-looking ultrasound device for the doctor's use; afterward slathering my breast with gel before the doctor came in and took the device from her. She patted my hand and looked at me reassuringly. "Shall we begin?"

"Whenever you're ready, I'm just along for the ride," I said in a kidding tone that I didn't really feel. I wanted her to be at ease as she examined me.

Quickly, we could see the egg-sized tumor in front, plus another golf ball-sized growth directly behind it and then a mass of deepest, darkest malevolence, which wound far down into the armpit. The entire evil mess was crisscrossed with tiny, newly birthed veins, malicious traitors, like small blood highways feeding the pulsing tumors. She told me she would have to do a number of biopsies and asked if I was up to that. I told her to do whatever she needed to do.

Eighteen biopsies turned my left breast into what looked like a couple pounds of hamburger meat. The nurse taped me together as best she could, shaking her head all the while, and I was led back to a dressing room. Left to change into my street clothes, I felt drained and helpless, so I plopped down on the small bench and attempted, without much success, to pull my shirt over my head.

Doc had told me she was sorry, it would probably take forty-eight to seventy-two hours to get results back on my samples, and we likely wouldn't know anything until after the weekend. I was so sore I just wanted to crawl into a hole and pull the hole in after me.

Still trying hopelessly to wriggle into my shirt, without proper use of my left arm, suddenly there was a sharp rap on the door and the doctor's voice asking if she could come in. I stood to open the door and the look on her face told me the news was not good. I sat back down on the dressing room's bench as she explained that the lab tech had taken my samples across the street, put my tissues on slides, and added the appropriate solution, which caused the biopsy fragments to almost leap off the glass slides.

We didn't need seventy-two or even forty-eight hours to know the results. I was harboring a very virulent and fast-growing cancer, which seemed to be of great concern to her. She told me we needed to move very quickly; there was no time to lose. Insisting a surgical procedure was the only way to begin and that she'd already called around to see if there was a surgeon who could see me the next morning for a consult, I was terrified, scared beyond reason. Approaching my husband in the waiting room with misty eyes and a quivering lip, he stood and held me.

My meeting with the surgeon Friday morning was every bit as filled with urgency and fearful expectation as the appointment the previous day had been, and my stress level flew through the roof. My husband was in panic mode as well. We wanted to do what would give me the best survival chances. The surgeon insisted it was imperative we move as quickly as possible, just as the previous doctor had urged, so surgery was set for the following Monday, only three days away.

As we drove home that morning, I took in the splendor of the beautiful fall landscape and wondered if this would be the last time I'd ever see the soybean fields change colors from green to yellow, to gold and rust. Marty and I had often talked about a road trip we wanted to take to watch fall leaves changing colors, beginning in Maine and all the way down the Eastern seaboard, and suddenly, it didn't seem very likely that trip would ever take place.

We went home and talked to our grown daughter Liz. She cried. We all prayed together, asking God to heal me. Liz was an ardent believer. She reminded me of a decade earlier when she'd had a very serious close call with her own health, and we'd prayed with her and anointed her with oil. She knew God heard our prayers and healed her. How could I still have doubt?

As I said before, I really didn't question there is a God, or even that He healed others, especially my beautiful daughter and my deserving husband, but I couldn't wrap my mind around the idea that He might do it solely and only for my sake.

I was so sure I didn't deserve anything good that my mind was made up whether God liked it or not. My guilt and the weight of condemnation smothered me. I knew all the evil things I'd done in my life, the terrible thoughts I'd had when I wished the people dead who'd hurt me as a child; people who'd later died; I was sure due to my evil thoughts and wishes. And, what about the vile things that were done to me for so many years? Surely, God couldn't ignore that. I must certainly be filthy and disgusting in His perfect and holy sight.

I told Marty I couldn't bear to call anyone else that day. Certainly, that would be something we could do after a good night's rest and some additional reflection. What a joke, a good night's rest. Next morning, I walked and cried, then we spent the day calling family and friends asking for prayer and trying to sound braver than we felt. Marty, Liz, and I prayed together again and Marty once again anointed me with oil, but it didn't soothe my fears. I expected to feel something, as I had when we'd anointed Liz, but I knew I wasn't worthy of His time and wondered why anyone thought He would waste His effort on me. In my mind, it was one thing to pray for healing for a church member or family, but completely a different matter to pray for myself.

I'd been made most of my life to feel insignificant and unworthy by so many people that overcoming a pervasive sense of shame and humiliation would be one of my biggest obstacles in this coming battle.

UNDESERVED GRACE

In June of 2010, just five months before my November diagnosis, my husband and I began to read and study more about the idea of radical grace through faith in Jesus's sacrifice for us. We'd barely begun to scratch the surface of the implications of a grace so powerful, and, I have to admit, Marty was catching on much more quickly than I. This is a grace, through faith, which is already absolute and available to all those who believe, complete with all the miraculous blessings which accompany that wonderful free gift.

We were very, very slowly coming to understand the meaning of grace in the person of Jesus Christ, who already paid the price of not only our salvation, but also our healing, our prosperity, our deliverance, and our mental peace on the cross at Calvary.

It's a difficult grace to comprehend when you've been taught, as we both had our entire lives, that you must accept Jesus as your personal Savior to assure your eternal home, but then once you are saved, there is a list of rules and regulations you must keep if you want to sustain your own salvation. That idea of maintaining my salvation was a very difficult one for me, as I had felt like a screwup since I was a small child. How could I, an imperfect mess, maintain perfection? I didn't say it out loud to my family, or to members of our church, but I knew I was doomed to an eternity in hell if any part of my salvation depended on my actions.

We were recently learning that the Word of God tells a very different story than the one we'd been force-fed as children, but we were also having a hard time letting go of that wrong way of thinking and adjusting ourselves to a life free from the guilt and expectations of the law, which had previously weighed us down. When things went wrong in my life, I automatically assumed I was receiving my "just rewards" for all the terrible things I'd done. Even though I'd asked Jesus to be my Savior, I still felt I needed to pay for every sin I'd ever committed, usually over and over again. I was trying to gain my worth through works. I didn't understand the true meaning of faith or grace.

Paul poses a great question in Galatians 3:1–5. He wants to know how the Galatians could believe they were saved by faith one minute and then go back to believing they were made righteous by works of the law the next. After much study and prayer, I eventually realized I was making the same mistake.

> O foolish Galatians! Who has bewitched you? It was before your eyes that Jesus Christ was publicly portrayed as crucified. Let me ask you only this; did you receive the Spirit by works of the law or by hearing with faith? (Gal. 3:1–2, ESV)

He called them fools for thinking they could finish a thing in the flesh, which was begun in the spirit and reminds them that Abraham believed and it was counted to him as righteousness.

> Are you so foolish? Having begun by the Spirit, are you now being perfected by the flesh? Did you suffer so many things in vain—if indeed it was in vain? Does He who supplies the Spirit to you and works miracles among you do so by works of the law or by hearing with faith, just as Abraham believed God, and it was counted to him as righteousness. (Gal. 3:3–6, ESV)

In Galatians 3:10, Paul tells us that those who rely on works are actually cursed, and in verse 11, he reminds us that the righteous live by faith.

> For all who rely on works of the law are under a curse; for it is written, "Cursed be everyone who does not abide by all things written in the Book of the Law, and do them." Now it is evident that no one is justified before God by the law, for "The righteous shall live by faith." But the law is not faith, rather "The one who does them shall live by them." (Gal. 3:10–12, ESV)

Then Paul reminds us in verses 13 and 14 that Jesus took our curse upon Himself so that we can have the Spirit through faith! I needed that same reminder of Christ's promise to me.

> Christ redeemed us from the curse of the law by becoming a curse for us–for it is written, "Cursed is everyone who is hanged on a tree," so that in Christ Jesus the blessing of Abraham might come to the Gentiles, so that we might receive the promised Spirit through faith. (Gal. 3:13–14, ESV)

That "legalistic" mentality, which captured and held the Galatians in its grip, kept me prisoner my whole life up to that point; since childhood, I had been trying to *prove myself worthy* of that free gift. But, if I am worthy, or gain worthiness by my own actions, and have earned my place, then the gift is no longer a gift is it? Could it be true that He loves me so much I don't need to earn His love and acceptance? Paul makes this point abundantly clear in his letter to the Romans.

> Therefore since we have been justified by faith, we have peace with God through our Lord Jesus Christ. Through Him we have also obtained access by faith into this grace

in which we stand, and we rejoice in hope of the glory of God. More than that, we rejoice in our sufferings, knowing that suffering produces endurance, and endurance produces character, and character produces hope, and hope does not put us to shame, because God's love has been poured into our hearts through the Holy Spirit who has been given to us. (Rom. 5:1–5, ESV)

Yes, even while I was yet too weak to know what I needed, but only knew I was a sinner, He sacrificed Himself for me to provide me with reconciliation to God.

For while we were still weak, at the right time Christ died for the ungodly. For one will scarcely die for a righteous person-though perhaps for a good person one would dare even to die, but God shows His love for us in that while we were still sinners, Christ died for us. Since, therefore, we have now been justified by His blood, much more shall we be saved by Him from the wrath of God. For if while we were enemies we were reconciled to God by the death of His Son, much more, now that we are reconciled, shall we be saved by His life. More than that, we also rejoice in God through our Lord Jesus Christ, through whom we have now received reconciliation." (Rom. 5:6–11, ESV)

So, to get this straight, while I was still a sinner, Christ died for me. He didn't wait for me to clean up my act and become good enough in God's sight. *His sacrifice made me good enough in Him!* Wow, as long as I have trusted Jesus and believe in Him as my Lord and Savior, His act of unselfish love justifies me in the eyes of the Father? What a concept! The whole thought of unconditional love was unfamiliar to me.

Paul reminds the Romans in chapter 5 that they are not sinners because they sin, they sin because they are sinners. Through Adam's sin, we are all guilty, and through Christ's sacrifice, we are all redeemed if we believe on Him.

Therefore, just as sin came into the world through one man, and death through sin, and so death spread to all men because all sinned— for sin indeed was in the world before the law was given, but sin is not counted where there is no law. Yet death reigned from Adam to Moses, even over those whose sinning was not like the transgression of Adam, who was a type of the one who was to come.

But the free gift is not like the trespass. For if many died through one man's trespass, much more have the grace of God and the free gift by the grace of that one man Jesus Christ abounded for many. And the free gift is not like the result of that one man's sin. For the judgment following one trespass brought condemnation, but the free gift following many trespasses brought justification. For if, because of one man's trespass, death reigned through that one man, much more will those who receive the abundance of grace and the free gift of righteousness reign in life through the one man Jesus Christ. (Rom. 5:12–17, ESV)

While I was reading in chapter 5 of Romans, I was reminded, by Paul, that if I am not in Christ, I am condemned. If I am in Him, I'm justified and forgiven, thereby giving me eternal life in

Christ! *Why*, I wondered, *would anyone choose to be condemned?*

> Therefore, as one trespass led to condemnation for all men, so one act of righteousness leads to justification and life for all men. For as by the one man's disobedience the many were made sinners, so by the one man's obedience the many will be made righteous. Now the law came in to increase the trespass, but where sin increased, grace abounded all the more, so that, as sin reigned in death, grace also might reign through righteousness leading to eternal life through Jesus Christ our Lord. (Rom. 5:18–21, ESV)

I have to admit though that even while all the forgiveness and justification sounded wonderful, I was still confused! So, the law that I was taught as a kid, the law that I was ordered to follow by my childhood pastor, is it bad? No, the Bible tells us, of course, the law is not bad. The law was created by God for a purpose; and as long as the law is used for the purpose it was intended, it is good.

In 1 Timothy chapter 1, Paul explains that the law is good and was created for the ungodly and for sinners to show them the error of their ways.

> Now we know that the law is good, if one uses if lawfully, understanding this, that the law is not laid down for the just but for the lawless and disobedient, for the ungodly and sinners, for the unholy and profane, for those who strike their fathers and mothers, for murderers, the sexually immoral, men who practice homosexuality, enslavers, liars, perjurers, and whatever else is contrary to sound doctrine, in accordance with the gospel of the glory of the blessed God with which I have been entrusted. (1 Tim. 1:8–11, ESV)

Paul then thanks Jesus for judging him faithful through His love and for the mercy he has received through His love.

> I thank Him who has given me strength, Christ Jesus our Lord, because He judged me faithful, appointing me to His service, though formerly I was a blasphemer, persecutor, and insolent opponent. But I received mercy because I had acted ignorantly in unbelief,

WHEN ALL ELSE FAILS

and the grace of our Lord overflowed for me with the faith and love that are in Christ Jesus. (1 Tim. 1:12–14, ESV)

The more I read and studied, the more questions I had and the more I felt I had to read and study in order to understand. For, even Scriptures that were becoming more clear now, were still somewhat confusing; after all, I'd been led to believe they meant something entirely different for so many years prior to that time. Was this new interpretation the correct one? As I said, Marty was "getting it" much quicker than I was (I have a smart husband), so I came to him with questions; sometimes quite angry at the implications, and he tried to explain. I wasn't a very quick learner on this subject, I believe due to the amount of shame and guilt I'd carried throughout my lifetime. Forgiven felt almost wrong, as if I'd not paid quite enough yet, for all my former sin.

"So, then, I am righteous in Christ? Since He is in me and I am in Him and He is righteous, when God looks at me all He sees is Jesus? How can that be? I've never measured up. I've always sinned and fallen short. As a child in Pastor Brown's church, I was told I had to follow all the laws and commandments, and I know I haven't done that. I mess up every day! Yes, I asked Jesus to be my Savior, but that kind of unconditional love still seems completely impossible to me. I mean, it isn't okay to sin is it?" Well, the answer to that is, of course not!

I have never found a Scripture that gives us permission to sin. Paul is telling us that though we have sinned, we are forgiven through Jesus's sacrifice. If we are in Christ, that love we are living in Christ will work within us, changing us into new creatures that will no longer desire to sin because we are so grateful for His sacrifice. He is patient with us as we are becoming new creatures. As this change is taking place, Jesus acts as our advocate with the Father when we do sin.

"But all the evil things I've done in my past. I feel so condemned. Don't I have to pay for all that I did before I came to trust Christ as Savior? I mean, I did those things before I asked for forgiveness. Surely, He doesn't forgive all those terrible things too? And what about future sins, how are they covered?" The answer to that question is that all the sins you have ever committed were future sins to Christ when you committed them, because Jesus died and rose again two thousand years ago. And when He says you are forgiven, He means of every sin you have ever committed and every sin you will ever commit. What a Savior!

This passage in Romans is so liberating! It tells us that we are no longer condemned if we believe in Jesus! Jesus has fulfilled the law for us by taking our sin to the cross and paying it all! Every single bit of it!

> There is therefore now no condemnation for those who are in Christ Jesus. For the law of the spirit of life has set you free in Christ Jesus from the law of sin and death. For God has done what the law, weakened by the flesh, could not do. By sending His own Son in the likeness of sinful flesh and for sin, He condemned sin in the flesh, in order that the righteous requirement of the law might be fulfilled in us. (Rom. 8:1–4, esv)

At this point in my journey, even with boundless scriptural proof, I still did not have a full enough understanding of that grace so succinctly described in Romans 8, and I was functioning to a large degree in my ever familiar fear mode. I can be pretty stubborn, and I've always been told that if something sounds too good to be true it probably is. Well, this whole forgiven thing sounded better than anything I've ever heard before. How could any of this be true?

Perhaps the remorse of my inevitable humanity weighed me down, or maybe there is a certain amount of comfort that we find in a familiar thing, even if that thing we are putting our trust in is dead wrong. Guilt is one of those things.

Fear

Early Monday morning, on the day of my surgery, my husband and two of our dear pastor friends offered prayer over the surgeon's hands as the orderly wheeled me away. I was trying so hard to be brave that I piped up with a small joke, leaving those waiting with a smile on their lips, but inside I was trembling and terrified. Due to shadows which had also been detected in my right breast and in order to be perfectly safe, the surgeon performed a double mastectomy with a radical removal of seventeen lymph nodes, and lots of tissue, on the left side. When I woke later to a room full of family and friends, I felt as if I'd been run over by a truck and really did not want company.

Horribly sick from the anesthesia and morphine, and not wanting to bother the nurses, I wrestled with drainage tubes to get to the restroom in time to vomit. I found myself struggling with the question, "Where is God in all this?" I still had not come to fully understand the need to put my complete trust and faith in Him, and I continued to wallow in a prison of terror and self pity. Not yet grown enough in my walk to look back and see all the times in my life He'd been there to save me, to lift me up, and to keep me from destroying myself, I was sure I was finished.

Truthfully, I know I was just waiting to see how my situation would work out before I could break down and trust Him. Too frightened to let go of that disturbing yet familiar sense of worry, I guess I was leaning on the old adage that it sometimes seems the devil we know is preferable to the devil we don't know. What I didn't understand then was if I already knew the answers, if I already knew how things were going to work out, then where was the need for hope and faith? Faith is, after all, believing in something we cannot see.

Judy, a pastor friend, and breast cancer survivor herself, told me later when I'd confessed of my continual hesitation during that stressful time; that God opens the prison doors, but we still have to pick ourselves up and walk through them. God doesn't promise we won't have troubles, only that He will be with us as we go through those troubles. Our lives in this world, as Christians, will be filled with tribulation, but the good news is Christ has overcome the world!

Jesus' words in John 16:33 make it clear to us that as His followers, because we are in Him, we have nothing at all to worry about!

> I have said these things to you, that in me you may have peace. In the world you will have tribulation. But take heart; I have overcome the world. (John 16:33, ESV)

What a comfort this is when we come to a place of total trust.

After several complications, another surgery to stop excessive bleeding and a longer stay in the hospital than I'd anticipated; my husband was sitting in my room with me when the surgeon came in to give us news about lab results on the lymph nodes they'd removed during surgery. He informed us that fourteen of the seventeen nodes were positive for cancer. I looked at my husband and then back to the doctor and said, "So that's good, right? I mean that three of them were okay? That can't be all bad then, it must be a good sign."

Doc said, "Mrs. Young, this isn't a glass half full kind of situation. You must be one of those wide-eyed optimists. Understand that if even one lymph node is positive, the cancer has likely spread to other parts of your body. And, with fourteen lymph nodes positive, well, it just doesn't look very good at all, but we'll have to wait till you go in for your PET scans next month before we'll know just how bad it is." Then, he turned and left.

Months later, Marty and I talked and joked about the surgeon's lack of bedside manner, but at that moment, we could only sit and stare at each other in stunned silence over his defeatist pronouncement—an announcement that hung in the air like a dark cloud. His words sounded so grave, and now we would be forced to wait for a whole month, until I was healed enough from surgery to undergo further testing, before we'd know anything concrete. The sentence seemed inhumane. I was released the following day to go home and resume my life. I felt like half a woman and I hurt a great deal, not able to use my arms. All my life I'd been one of those people who took care of everyone else; I didn't know how to ask for help, or even how to accept it gracefully, if it was offered, and I just didn't seem to know how to get back to normal.

I pretended pretty well though, for anyone who was watching, to be strong in faith; but my faith wasn't yet half as strong as I let on to the world. Oh, I was trying! Believe me I was trying, but the harder I tried, the more I struggled. I know Marty was getting the whole idea of a grace, which didn't have to be earned, much quicker than I was, but I couldn't admit how weak my own faith was, not to him, and not to those who counted on us to be their spiritual leaders. I fully believed at that time I was going to die, and I felt pretty darned sorry for myself.

During the daytime, while Marty was at work and the house empty, I sat in my kitchen alone and cried. I doubted and questioned God's love for me; after all, I didn't deserve it, so why should I expect to receive it? Instead of praying and believing in His undeserved favor, I continued to wallow in fright and unbelief. I made the mistake of going online to find out more about my particular variety of cancer and the corresponding survival rates and was stunned by the wealth of negative information to be found. That foray onto the internet confirmed my worst fears, I would certainly die. There was a less than 5 percent chance of survival from this variety of cancer once the disease metastasized.

Still not truthful with my family, I didn't want them to know how weak my faith was. I was so ashamed over my lack of conviction; and that disgrace, added to all the humiliation of life's trials, along with the indignity of my childhood abuses battered my weary soul. Once all that guilt and shame multiplied in my mind, it caused me to believe that no matter what the Word said, I was singularly, completely unworthy of God's love and grace. Even if He wanted to save me, it wouldn't matter; I deserved to die.

On my second day home, I got a call from a nice lady at the hospital checking to see how I was getting along. She wanted to know what surgery I'd had, and when I told her about the number of lymph nodes that came back positive, she gasped. She shared about her cousin who'd had only three positive lymph nodes and who'd passed away several months back. Listening to her talk, I could hear the sound of nails being pounded into my proverbial coffin somewhere in the distance, and the fear grew exponentially.

Up to the point in my life in which somebody told me I had cancer, I'd always felt pretty darn strong. I'd been through a myriad of tragic events in my life—sexual and physical abuse among other things—and I'd survived them all, I supposed erroneously, by my own wit and strength. I felt, however mistakenly,

I could take on anything the world threw at me without batting an eye.

It's true that I was feeling strong in myself and not strong in the Lord since I didn't really have a close relationship with God at that point. And it is true, as I have since discovered that strength without the Lord is not real strength at all. But, false or not, I did feel like a strong, capable, intelligent woman all by myself. I was so sure of my own strength I frequently said, "I don't need anyone!" often in anger and even to my wonderful husband Marty during the first years of our marriage, who always looked wounded when those words spewed from my mouth.

Many told me that due to my traumatic childhood, I had every right to be angry, but I'd always claimed to be a victor. My proclamation of faith went something like this: "We can be victims of our circumstances, or we can be victors over our circumstances. I choose to be a victor." I'd spouted that declaration to many people in their moments of trial or grief; you know, supposedly to be an example to one who is weaker than I.

The problem was that I was putting my faith for victory in myself, not in my awesome Creator. A truth I've come to recognize is that God will not allow us to steal His glory forever, and He will allow my proverbial "bubble" to be popped if it is standing in the way of a true relationship with Him.

Several days after my return home from surgery when my daughter was busy elsewhere and wasn't able to help me get through my shower. Marty and I stood, a bit uncomfortably, in the bathroom. He was helping me dry off and dress, and I felt embarrassed for him to see my mangled, misshapen chest covered with bruises and staples. With misty eyes, he told me he loved me and that I would always be beautiful to him, then he wrapped his arms around me and we cried together for a good long time. I am so very blessed to be married to this man. He is truly my hero.

Upon hearing the doctor's news on November 4, we were all understandably shocked. Well, my family was shocked anyway. They reasoned, "We prayed for the surgery to be successful, didn't we? There are hundreds perhaps thousands of people all over the country praying for us, aren't there?" Their confused question then was, "Has God deserted us?"

I was ashamed to admit to my husband how weak my own faith was, that I'd known all along I didn't deserve God's help and that I didn't believe I deserved to be healed; hadn't believed it from the beginning, so none of this was as shocking to me as it was to them.

Marty told me afterward that he wondered if he was praying incorrectly; he said he thought he must be doing something wrong and he was sorry, so there was doubt there too. I felt badly that he believed he was doing something wrong. I'd suspected I was the only one who felt completely inept. He'd assumed it had something to do with his ability as a pastor, or husband, and was willing to take on the guilt for my situation. Was God even paying attention to us? Why was He allowing this, or worse, causing this to happen? I was especially angry at Him for allowing my husband to feel so guilty and condemned. We were utterly lost.

Marty asked me months later. "Would you have endured the double mastectomy if you'd known the cancer already spread and an operation wasn't going to get rid of it all?" Truthfully, I don't think I would have sacrificed my breasts, though they were well used after nursing all my children, if the surgery wasn't going to make a difference; and again, I began to second-guess every decision we'd made.

Why hadn't we prayed to find out what God's will was in all this before proceeding? We'd let panic and fear set in, and we'd been ruled by what the doctors wanted to do instead of going first to the one with all the answers, the Great Physician. How could we expect Him to do anything for us when our own faith had been so weak?

BEGINNING TO SEE THE LIGHT

As I sat again at my kitchen table one day feeling very much alone, I realized that something in my heart ached to have a true connection to the Lord. I'd always loved Him; since I was a little girl, I'd loved Him. True, it was in a frightened, far off way, but I did love Him. I'd just never felt in my wounded, broken heart that the love was reciprocated. I wanted finally to be able to live the Scriptures I'd been reading, but not altogether believing since we'd begun studying this message of grace.

I wanted to know how I could incorporate those powerful words into my fractured life. All the excuses I'd made over the years for not seeking the Lord; too busy, not enough time, too many demands on my schedule; came back to nudge me and I realized the only reason I didn't have the kind of relationship I desired with my God was because I had never made time for Him.

A stirring began, which I am convinced came directly from Him as do all good and wonderful things and a little of the studying we'd been doing started to sink in to my heart and mind and began to make sense. In a flash of true cognition, I realized for the first time that none of this was about what I do or how good I am. I'd been confusing *who* I am with *whose* I am. Nothing of what had happened, or ever would happen, had to do with whether or not I deserved it, or am worthy or not worthy enough. It is all about Him! He already did it all, and if I am in Him and He is in me, then I get what He gets because He deserves it, not because I do. I can never do enough to be worthy of His grace, but that's okay, because He is already worthy for me, and He has already fought these battles and won! As long as Jesus is my Lord and Savior, I am a conqueror, a victor—"It is finished." He deserves *all* the glory forever and ever. Amen! I was rocked to the core by this heart revelation.

> No, in all these things we are more than conquerors through Him who loved us (Rom. 8:37, ESV).

The problem of my healing, or lack of it, had never been God's problem. The problem was mine. He had not put impossible expectations on me. I had done that by trying to be faithful to an old school master—an old master who had served his purpose and was no longer of any value to me, the law. The law is good for what it was intended. God designed it to show us the depravity of our sin and convince us how desperately we need a savior, so in that regard, the law is good. But once we have come to the realization that we cannot be good enough on our own, and we decide to trust Jesus with our life and eternity, the law becomes a bog of death for our spiritual well-being. After we are born again to life in Christ, we are no longer under law, but under grace! We no longer want to do the childish things we desired to do in our spiritual youth. Now we want to do the right thing because of what He has already done for us. Not to gain our salvation, no, but in gratitude for it. That radical grace was the powerful, lifesaving element I had denied myself for all the decades of my life to this point.

In Romans 3:21 and 22, Paul tells us that God has come in the person of Jesus, apart from the law, and that if we believe, our faith makes us righteous.

> But now the righteousness of God has been manifested apart from the law, although the Law and the Prophets bear witness to it—the righteousness of God through faith in Jesus Christ for all who believe. For there is no distinction. (Rom. 3:21–22, ESV)

In verses 23, 24, and 25, we see that all have sinned and that grace is a free gift from God to be received by faith in Jesus.

> For all have sinned and fall short of the glory of God, and are justified by His Grace as a gift, through the redemption that is in Christ Jesus, whom God put forward as a propitiation by His blood, to be received by faith. This was to show God's righteousness,

because in His divine forbearance He had passed over former sins. (Rom. 3:23–25, esv)

Then in verse 26, Paul shows us that in God's righteousness He is just and that He has the right to justify any who has faith in Jesus.

It was to show His righteousness at the present time, so that He might be just and the justifier of the one who has faith in Jesus. (Rom. 3:26, esv)

Glory to God! I used to try so hard to be holy on my own, not realizing that the holier I tried to act by doing works that might impress those around me, the further I pushed the Lord away.

In Ephesians chapter 2, we see that it is Christ who draws us near, by His blood, and Christ who brings peace and tears down walls. Through Him, we are no longer strangers and in fact are being made His dwelling place!

But now in Christ Jesus you who once were far off have been brought near by the blood of Christ. For He Himself is our peace, who has made us both one and has broken down in His flesh the dividing wall of hostility by abolishing the law of commandments expressed in ordinances, that He might create in Himself one new man in place of the two, so making peace, and might reconcile us both to God in one body through the cross, thereby killing the hostility. And He came and preached peace to you who were far off and peace to those who were near. For through Him we both have access in one Spirit to the Father. So then you are no longer strangers and aliens, but you are fellow Citizens with the saints and members of the household of God, built on the foundation of the apostles and prophets, Christ Jesus Himself being the cornerstone, in whom the whole structure being joined together grows into a holy temple in the Lord. In Him you also are being built together into a dwelling place for God by the Spirit. (Eph. 2:13–22, ESV)

Some might say that cancer is an evil, terrible monster, but if not for cancer, I would not have come to know His grace in such a personal way. Cancer could easily have become my "yoke of slavery," but I no longer believe that God causes *bad* things to happen in our lives, or that He merely sits back and watches us flounder. I do believe He allows situations and circumstances to come into our lives to help us grow in our faith, but now I believe due to His sacrifice on the cross, disease cannot live in this body when it is filled with eternal life in Him, at least not for any extended period of time.

I recognize now God is simply waiting for us to quit trying to do it all through our own efforts, and He desires that we would ask Him for help. He is our helper, our creator, and the one who loves us most. He was always here in my life and wanting to help, but had to wait for me to quit trying to earn salvation, healing, deliverance, and peace on my own and get out of His way. He simply cannot work for me when I am trying to do it all on my own. When I work, He rests; when I rest in Him, He works.

> So then, there remains a Sabbath rest for the people of God, for whoever has entered

God's rest has also rested from his works as God did from His" (Heb. 4:9–10, ESV).

In Romans 8:28, Paul reveals that if we are believers, God will work all things together for our good. He alone has the power to effect true changes in my life. And in verse 31, we see that, with God on our side, who can be against us?

> And we know that for those who love God all things work together for good, for those who are called according to His purpose (Rom. 8:28, ESV).

> What then shall we say to these things? If God is for us, who can be against us? (Rom. 8:31, ESV).

That same day in which I felt a stirring in my spirit from the Lord, I began to search for and speak out loud, every positive, healing scripture I could find in my Bible. I stood in the middle of my kitchen several times a day saturating myself in these scriptures, speaking them over my wounded body and beginning to believe for the first time in my battered, mortal existence that each and every one of them were real, already finished, already true for me. Every time I prayed and spoke the healing scriptures, I felt better, stronger than before.

But I would be forced over the next few months, as Satan slithered around my mind and I vacillated back and forth between faith and doubt, trust and unbelief, to prayerfully consider the words which came out of my own mouth. I would begin to understand that with our own mouths we speak our personal destiny, and I would gradually learn to speak God's truth over my life instead of the doubt with which I still struggled and the fear I had lived out for so long.

> You are snared by the words of your mouth:
> you are taken by the words of your mouth
> (Prov. 6:2 , ESV).

We didn't tell our son Dave about my surgery right away. Not wanting him to have that knowledge weighing on him while he was going through combat training, with live ammunition flying over his head, we felt it was information better saved for another time. After his combat training was complete and before he would go on to MOS schooling, the Red Cross contacted his superiors and he was sent home for a visit. I think we were all so sure the surgery was successful in clearing out all the disease that the words of the doctor on that fourth of November came as a complete shock to us all. One, I certainly hadn't been prepared for my son to hear before he would be leaving us again so soon.

I was brand-new to this positive way of believing, and it was unfortunately still easy for me to be swept away into moments of despair. It would take all of God's effort on my behalf to help me finally stop worrying and learn to trust Him with my whole heart.

CHANGING MY CONFESSION

Old habits are difficult to break, and without being fully aware of it at the time, I continued trying to work out parts of my healing on my own, slipping back into old ways of thinking; instead of leaning completely on Him, I was trying to deserve my miracle. At first, truthfully, I might even have been keeping a mental tally of how many positive scriptures I quoted per day as if I was somehow paying the toll for the healing I might eventually receive.

I'd begun, in some distant part of my psyche, to realize God loves me and wants to heal me, but there was a bigger piece of me that still felt a need to earn everything I might receive from Him. I desperately needed to change my confession, but I would only be able to do that with His help, and as I said, I hated asking anyone for help.

As a self-proclaimed Christian, I'd always believed that my confession was a mental listing of my sins and all the faults that needed correcting in my life. For decades, every time I prayed, I asked for forgiveness of all my old sins, usually the same old sins over and over, though I was forever adding to that list. I don't know how you feel after you pray, but I never really quite felt "forgiven" if you know what I mean. I believed that until something happened to rid me of those feelings of guilt, God could not help me, and certainly, I didn't deserve His help. I'd not realized before that Christianity *is* our confession. Until I began delving into the grace message further, I didn't know our confession is the testimony of our faith in Christ, our agreement with God for the promises He has made to us as His beloved children. Our faith in the work that has already been accomplished; the work we don't need to try to do ourselves because "It is finished" once and for all. Once I began to understand that unique concept and stopped looking at my confession as a negative profession, things began to make a bit more sense.

> Let us hold fast the confession of our hope without wavering, for He who promised is faithful (Heb. 10:23, ESV).

After weeks of agreeing with God's Word over and over again throughout the day, my mind started just a tiny bit at a time to line up with the promises I was reading. Where before in my thinking the scriptures were just words, soon I began to see them as His Word and they took on a whole new meaning. I found myself beginning to believe those promises more and more, and instead of pretending to have faith in God's love and desire to care for me, I really started to feel His love covering me.

> The Lord is my shepherd; I shall not want (Ps. 23:1, ESV).

The more I read, the more I wanted to read, it wasn't a chore anymore. I couldn't wait to get up in the morning and learn more of His favor and grace. The more I discovered about His faithfulness, the more I trusted Him. The more I trusted Him, the more I believed His promises were for me. The doctor's prognosis had not changed. The results of the PET scans had not changed. But my mind began to evolve as I became filled with the faith of God, not just faith in God, but the faith of God, His knowledge, His grace.

My confession began to be one of trust in a creator God who had died for me and who loved me as if I was the only human living on earth. I don't mean that as a selfish thing. When we trust Him, He loves each of us as if we are the only human being on earth; and if you were the only person alive, He would still have died for you! I suddenly and gratefully began to experience peace for the first time in my life! When you have spent your life as a worry wart like I had, peace is a change quite desirable.

> Many are the afflictions of the righteous, but the Lord delivers him out of them all (Ps. 34:19, ESV).

It was very difficult to think of myself as "the righteous" until I began to see that my righteousness had nothing to do with me and only with Jesus's sacrifice for me.

Prayer was finally, thankfully, becoming an easy conversation with a loving Father. It took quite a long time to get to that point since I'd never really known a loving father before in my life. But once I learned to go to Him—with anything and everything—that conversation got ever easier, and I wondered how I had survived all the years of my life prior to this time without that fellowship. My prayer life before had been endless rambling about past sins, which I knew now He didn't even remember, and lists of selfish wants, as if perhaps God was nothing more than a great big Santa Claus in the sky.

Now my daily conversations with God began when I woke in the morning and ended as I fell asleep, usually in the middle of a sentence of gratitude.

> Rejoice always, pray without ceasing, give thanks in all circumstances, for this is the will of God in Christ Jesus for you (1 Thess. 5:16–18, ESV).

I'd never been so filled with joy. How could I be happy when I still had doctors telling me I had cancer? I will never be able to explain it to you any better than this: I'd turned my life over to the Lord wholly and completely. I'd finally come to a place where I totally trusted God; a place where I really believed His Word for me, not just for other people but for me, was true. He'd taught me how to talk to Him, and He'd filled me with the hope of the Holy Spirit, my heart was lighter because I no longer carried the weight of the world. I knew without a doubt that He was responsible for all of it. And, no matter the outcome, whatever He decided for me would ultimately be what was best for me. I couldn't take any credit, didn't want any credit and knew I didn't deserve it. Suddenly, I was no longer worried. My heart was filled with a peace I couldn't explain, but didn't need to!

> Do not be anxious about anything, but in everything by prayer and supplication with thanksgiving let your requests be made known to God. And the peace of God, which surpasses all understanding, will guard your

hearts and your minds in Christ Jesus. (Phil. 4:6–7, ESV)

I do have to say that once I really started to understand the implications of His undeserved grace, His unmerited favor, and His limitless love, I took off running with it. It freed me from decades of loneliness, guilt, shame, and wrong thinking and allowed me to open up to His desires and plans for my life. Now I wanted to be used by Him in more ways and to share His love with everyone I met. Thinking *right* thoughts began to translate into doing *right* things; not to deserve His love, but in gratitude for it!

Many people tried to tell me that we'd given up true Christianity to believe in a cheap grace, a grace that allows us to sin without feeling guilty and not be accountable for our actions. I could not disagree more. I don't believe there is such a thing as cheap grace. The price God paid in giving up His beloved Son for us and the price Jesus paid in His sacrifice on the cross cannot possibly be considered cheap. Compared to the blood of goats and bulls that paid the price of sin for a year in the Old Testament, the precious blood of Christ paid an eternal price for me, for us, for all who will believe.

> But when Christ appeared as a high priest of the good things that have come, then through the greater and more perfect tent (not made with hands, that is, not of this creation) He entered once for all into the holy places, not by means of the blood of goats and calves but by means of His own blood, thus securing an eternal redemption. For if the blood of goats and bulls, and the sprinkling of defiled persons with the ashes of a heifer, sanctify for the purification of the flesh, how much more will the blood of Christ, who through the eternal Spirit offered Himself without blemish to God, purify our conscience from dead works to serve the living God." (Heb. 9:11–14, ESV)

We were also told by many that if we continued teaching this cheap grace, we would fall from His grace. But we discovered that Paul, who encountered the same arguments, tells us the opposite is true; that if we try to justify ourselves through the law, we shall fall from grace.

> You are severed from Christ, you who would
> be justified by the law; you have fallen away
> from grace (Gal. 5:4, ESV).

Now that I am not living under the condemnation of law, I know this new relationship I have with my Lord causes me to *not* want to sin, or go against what He desires for my life; not because I am trying to earn, or deserve His grace and love, but in sincere gratitude for what He has already done for me. Paul warns us not to allow the freedom He has given us to be an excuse to sin. I have never wanted to sin less than I do today and this when He has given me the freedom to do what I wish!

> For you were called to freedom, brothers. Only
> do not use your freedom as an opportunity for
> the flesh, but through love serve one another.
> For the whole law is fulfilled in one word:
> "You shall love your neighbor as yourself."
> (Gal. 5:13–14, ESV)

What I desire today is to love people and to share the love of Christ with everyone I meet! How can anyone be given the best gift in the universe, the gift of life through Jesus Christ, and not want to share it with the world? I am certainly not perfect, but He is perfect and is working on me and in me, to bring me to the fullness of Christ. I want everyone in the world to experience that marvelous gift!

Following my surgery and the not so positive prognosis, many friends, family, and even other pastors spoke defeat over me, without realizing it, with words such as, "Well, whatever the will of God is. If He wants you to be healed, you will be. But if He wants you home with Him, that will be the way of it," and "God doesn't promise to heal us here on earth now does He," and "Sometimes, our healing happens on the other side." At first, I'd passively agreed with them, knowing that all things which happen do certainly pass through His hands. Words like, "Well, we never know what God's will is," were rampant. But I have come to disagree wholeheartedly with that statement. We do know what God's will is for us, as it is clearly stated in His

Word. His will for us is to have life and to have it more abundantly!

After more reading and studying, Marty and I concluded we could not find a single place in the Bible where someone came to Jesus believing for healing and He turned them away! So that was His plan for me, a plan for healing. The key word then was and today is *believe*, and the key attitude was and is the knowledge that my healing is already accomplished once and for all!

This is not a healing that we are waiting for one day, but one which was already paid for and taken care of two thousand years ago. His Word says, "With thanksgiving, let your requests be known to God." With thanksgiving! So, previously when we'd begged for healing that might be done someday, our prayers fell like stones, but when we began to thank Him, believing the requests are already fulfilled, as He said they are, we were then speaking His will over our lives.

We decided then and there that no matter what the world declares, we will declare that He loves us and since we came to Him believing it was only a matter of time before we would see the physical manifestation of the healing He had promised; the healing we believed had already taken place. No matter what the facts of the scans were, we would believe the truth. Nothing would dissuade us from that hard fought knowledge! And I felt better emotionally than I had in a very long time.

> But He was wounded for our transgressions;
> He was crushed for our iniquities; upon Him
> was the chastisement that brought us peace,
> and by His stripes we are healed (Isa. 53:5,
> ESV).

Due to those continual negative scan results and the "proof" that existed, everyone—from some of our distant family to so-called friends, other pastors, many doctors and nurses and most of our neighbors—thought we were completely crazy to believe I was already healed. As a matter of fact, my doctor, even made little jokes about me for being so determined in my faith and my expectation of a physical manifestation of miraculous healing. I had finally begun to have faith, a faith which could not be shaken!

> Now faith is the assurance of things hoped for, the conviction of things not seen (Heb. 11:1, ESV).

I was starting to see the value in seeking the face of God; the value of hope, the importance of unwavering faith. I desired, more than anything in the world, to please Him.

> And without faith it is impossible to please Him, for whoever would draw near to God must believe that He exists and that He rewards those who seek Him (Heb. 11:6, ESV).

I had nothing to offer my doctor by way of proof except for the scriptures I'd been believing, so I stood on those, but he continued trying to get me to see reason. After all, he surmised, I should make provisions for my family, no matter the outcome. And, as human beings from every sector of my life, many of whom professed Christ as Savior, continued to speak death over me, God continued to speak life, and I held on to His truth, the only truth. I know now that there are proclaiming Christians and possessing Christians, and we must possess Christ to be able to completely trust in His Word.

MY MESS

I suppose it's really not so odd that I'd grow up confused as I'm sure many others did in a world of mixed messages. Our lives are bombarded with so many points of view, religious and otherwise. Popular world view has changed much over these past fifty years or so, and Christianity has become less fashionable in our own culture and persecuted unto death in many others. As we are inundated with threats of "hate crimes" for quoting Scripture, or for disagreeing with another's religious outlooks, some wonder if it is worth it to stand for what is right. My own confusion was a result of many things.

Two days after my fourth birthday, I lay writhing on the cool floor of the hallway in our Northern California home. I was in severe pain, and my parents stepped back and forth over me ignoring me at my dad's insistence. My father, who'd been disappointed when I was born a girl, instead of the son he wanted, was sure I was simply throwing a tantrum. My mother who swore I'd never thrown a fit in my entire four years of life finally became extremely concerned and subjected herself to his ire by calling our family doctor. An ambulance ride to the hospital and surgery to remove a burst appendix proved her right. He had largely overlooked my existence up to that point as he lavished my older sister with whatever strange, conditional type of love he possessed, but that incident seemed to change something in him. It was as if I'd embarrassed him by daring to actually be sick when he'd claimed I wasn't. He'd always hated being proved wrong, and I paid very dearly for that day going forward.

I was a precocious child, picking up on things more quickly than many of my peers; and from that point on, my mere existence seemed to annoy him. My grandmother told me she thought he was so different with me than he was with my siblings because I reminded him of him as a child. He must have loathed himself if that were actually the case. He was a brilliant man who grew up in a Jewish household with a father who abused him; a fact I didn't discover until after he passed away when I was already an adult.

He hated his father's god—a god of anger and rules—and became a hard and fast atheist when he left home at the age of seventeen to join the Marines and serve on the Pacific front in World War II. He later served in the Korean conflict and then as a military advisor at the beginning of the war in Vietnam. He carried so much rage, which could be due in part to his years in battle, but I'm sure was begun at home.

I became the sorry focus of his rage after my surgery. Thinking I was using my appendectomy scar to get the attention of my mother and insisting I do lots of extra chores because of it, he harassed me constantly to let me know how disappointed he was in me, pushing me and slapping me to help me get a move on. I'd become a fairly proficient reader by the age of three and found great solace in my books, but when he was angry, he took away my reading materials and kept them from me for days at a time.

I woke one night, a month after my appendix surgery, with a hand over my mouth. His hot alcohol-laden breath, stealing my air, left me struggling for breath. He raped me and left me crying, broken and bleeding, trembling in my bed.

My mother, who in those days was usually drunk by seven or eight in the evening—a condition which seemed to inoculate her from the truth of her married relationship—swore she didn't hear a thing. The next morning, I tried to tell her what happened, and she called me a liar, yelling obscenities at me, she slapped me so hard that I flew backward into the closet door. I got up holding my stinging, swollen face and ran from the room. I would never attempt to get help again. Learning very young that I couldn't count on anyone to protect me, I became aware and very self sufficient at a tender age.

For the rest of that summer and every night until I was nine and a half years old, my nights were filled with fright and unimaginable torture at his hands. Some nights, I would wake to him in my bed, after my mother would drink herself into a stupor; other nights, he would yank me from my bed and take me to the living room where he would beat me with his belt, for whatever supposed evils I might have committed that day.

I discovered that I could occasionally get away with crawling into bed with my younger sister to avoid him, and if he was drunk enough, he might not detect where I had hidden, but that didn't work often as she was a solid sleeper, and he would often find me there anyway and drag me back to my bed. Kicking and screaming didn't help. If I made him angry, I earned myself a beating along with whatever else he desired.

I started kindergarten that fall at only four years old. My reading skills had put me miles ahead of my peers, though my limited social skills would prove to be a stumbling block for me as I was advanced two more times throughout my elementary school years. I began to have ongoing stomach problems due to the constant stress of his mistreatment, and I started missing some school because of it. My beloved kindergarten teacher noticed some ugly bruises on my back and arms one day and said something to her superiors, but due to the fact that my father's family was well connected, I found myself rather quickly with a new teacher who seemed far less concerned about my well-being.

Night after night, I was abused in one way or another. One night, when I was six years old, he dragged me to the basement by my hair, where he and his cronies were playing cards, and he made me stand in the middle of the card table to sing "Over the Rainbow" for their entertainment. Tears ran down my face as I choked and sang while drunken men lifted my nightgown and grabbed at me.

I know my mother knew what was happening because there was ample evidence in the bed where he attacked me and because she began including me in more conversations of an adult nature, as if, even though I was only four, five, or six, I might have more insight now into those issues she was battling. Those talks continued for years.

Time and again, she took me aside and confided in me, as you might with another grown woman, about affairs my father was having with neighborhood women. She also described to me her own terrible and perverted sex life with my father. Crying on my shoulder for hours as she drank glass after glass of port wine, she poured out her fears and worries. I didn't tell her then, but I didn't care if he was having sex with others, because on those extracurricular nights, he might become tired enough to only beat me and not come to my bed and maybe even ignore me all together.

Strangely, I didn't hate my mother. As odd as it is to admit, there were even moments in my exhaustion that I felt special when she confided in me. It was the only feeling of relationship we shared. Never there for me when I needed her throughout my life, she didn't protect me as you might imagine a mother would, but I saw her instead as one who was weak and needed protection herself. Over the years, I came to look after her as best I could throughout all the terrible and unfortunate decisions she made.

Daughter of a Baptist minister, she'd stopped going to church when she left home to find fame and fortune as a model or actress, whichever came to fruition the most quickly. There were many stops and short-lived relationships, even a couple of marriages, along the way as she worked her way to California. She met and married my father rather quickly, as we discovered later that she'd been pregnant with my older sister Dawn before they wed.

She told me on multiple occasions, in which she was drunk as usual, that she wished I'd never been born. She didn't seem to say it as if she was trying to hurt me, but rather as a matter of fact. Her reasoning was that my birth had made my father angry since I wasn't the son he'd expected, and that put a wedge in their otherwise "perfect" relationship. Her confessions broke my heart, but they also gave me the steely resolve it took to take care of myself without help and eventually take care of my siblings where and when I could.

My mom's drinking grew worse and worse after my father went to prison for forgery when I was almost ten. She tried to cope with being lonely in her own broken way. One of the ways she soothed herself was to take over his penchant for torturing me. She called me awful names and slapped me in the face, or knocked me into the nearest wall whenever she felt I hadn't done a chore perfectly, or if her own private life was going poorly. If I answered back, I was backhanded, dragged to my room by my hair, or beat on the head and back with her hairbrush or fist.

From birth, I'd quite regularly suffered from ear infections. The summer I turned nine, I committed some infraction on her endless list, and as a punishment, she made me lay in a bathtub filled with ice water for hours. She sat by the door drinking, and every time I tried to get out of the tub, she pushed me back down. When she finally released me from my punishment, I promptly got a severe ear infection which ruptured my eardrums. Over time, she was so frustrated with my health that she began reacting as if I were at fault somehow for having yet another painful infection.

One night, when I was nine years old, I was bathing, and she came into the bathroom to talk to me. She was drunk as usual and was telling me I should just quit getting those stupid ear infections, after all they were such a huge inconvenience for her. I told her I wished I could stop getting them since they were painful, and I certainly disliked them more than she did. She grew angry with me as if perhaps I was disagreeing with her and was just refusing to stop being sick.

Suddenly, she grabbed my head and held me under the water. I struggled and thrashed about trying to get away. It was obvious she was trying to drown me, and I fought for my life. I was close to unconsciousness and losing strength quickly, but still she wouldn't let go. With the last of my might, I was forced to kick my way out. In the process, she was struck in the face.

I gave her a bloody nose when I kicked her, so as I was trying to climb out of the tub, choking and gasping for air, she picked up the small metal trash can next to the toilet and began hitting me over and over again until she couldn't raise her arms anymore. Finally, exhausted, she collapsed to the floor sobbing. I got out of the tub soaking wet, bloody and bruised and sat with her, rubbing her back and telling her that everything would be all right. My confused heart broke for her, but I never took a bath again without first locking the door.

On another occasion after my father was sent to prison and we four girls had started going to church with them on Sundays, we had Pastor Brown and his wife over for supper. Again my mother was drunk. I'd made baked pork chops, mashed potatoes, and peas for our meal. I'd taken over the majority of the cooking, the household chores, and the care of my younger siblings several years earlier, due to my mother's drinking and her listless and inattentive attitude.

Mother decided she wanted applesauce to complete the menu. Canned applesauce has always been a texture which is hard for me to stomach, and my nerves were already on edge due to the reality of our company and my mother's current state of intoxication.

During the meal, she insisted I eat my applesauce, and I told her I wasn't feeling very well and didn't know if I could. She got up and marched over to me—much to the horror of the Browns—and picked up a spoonful of applesauce, shoving it in my mouth and hitting my gag reflex. I retched and threw up on my plate. She became so livid that she proceeded to scoop up spoonfuls of the vomit and shovel it into my mouth. It took both Pastor and Mrs. Brown to pull her off me as I sobbed and gagged.

Loneliness for her absent husband consumed her, but with him gone, she began again to date. She started bringing men home and our situation grew worse. It seems pedophiles have radar which leads them to the homes of helpless children, and on more occasions than I can count, her dates would leave her drunk and sleeping in her own bed to come attack me in the middle of the night. I finally took to propping a chair under the doorknob of the children's bedroom to keep us safe.

Then there was the incident when I was in sixth grade and had earned the lead in our annual Christmas pageant. The play was about to begin and in walked my mother, stumbling all the way down the aisle. She removed her coat and had nothing on beneath it but a see-through negligee sans underwear. The school principal quickly got to her seat, pulled her coat back around her, and ushered her outside where he hurriedly drove her home. I was mortified as the other students and their parents stared and gossiped. There are many, many more stories I could share, but I'm sure you get the point by now.

Though I know in her own twisted way my mother loved us, her failure to achieve the goal of stardom that she so desperately sought when she was younger would eventually lead to a deep resentment of her children and a general hatred of life. Her world spiraled out of control over the years as alcohol claimed another victim, and she died a tragic, drunken, accidental death at only fifty-six years old.

My father detested even the name of God and was a very troubled man. The only god he knew was the angry god of his Jewish father, and he wanted nothing to do with him. After his death many years later, I was to discover the brutal ways his own father had physically and sexually abused him, and I mourned his innocence, feeling much sorrow for the torture he'd endured. I eventually learned to forgive him for the things he'd done to me in my childhood, and I called him to talk and offer my forgiveness about six months before he died alone of lung cancer. I tried to share Jesus with him at that time, but he wouldn't hear of it. He'd never told any of his children that he was sick, perhaps thinking no one would care to help after all he'd done; and my heart broke when I heard of his passing alone in his apartment. He wasn't found for several days.

His imprisonment when I was nine ended years of personal physical and sexual abuse by him in my childhood and stopped our family having to move around in order to escape the law, only to create a whole new set of problems caused by our mother's loneliness, alcoholism, and poor decisions.

She eventually married my stepfather who seemed to be a bright light in our lives for a short time, until a tour in Vietnam left him an angry, confused, alcoholic who fell right into my mom's cycle of booze and abuse. Soon after his return from overseas, they began to fight. Their arguments were loud and violent and always included plenty of alcohol. He never did find out she'd been unfaithful to him the entire year and a half he was overseas, and I couldn't bear to be the one to break his heart, so we didn't tell him that she left us all alone for days and weeks at a time to spend as much time as possible with her new boyfriend, even going on vacations with his family. During that time, I stepped up and cared for my siblings as usual. She continued to carry on a correspondence with her lover, behind her husband's back, until the day she died. Mail came for her after her death, which my stepdad opened, and though I'm sure he realized what had gone on all those years, he never said a word. Her lover even wrote to me to send me some of her things after he found out about her death.

I adored Pastor and Mrs. Brown, the pastors from our childhood church. They'd taken an interest in us after our father was sent to prison, and they visited our home frequently, or took us on little day outings. They saw the life our mother was living and volunteered to go out of their way to pick us up on Sundays. Collecting us girls in time to get us to the church before Sunday school started, we sat lined up in the backseat of their car. Years later, Pastor Brown would comment at my sister Dawn's funeral that he always loved looking into his backseat to see those four little pair of patent leather shoes lined up.

When we arrived, they would feed us breakfast, knowing no one else had bothered. Mrs. Brown always told us we should eat something so we wouldn't have any "rumblies in our tumblies" during services. I loved the Browns for the way they seemed to care about us in their own way. In that year of steady church attendance, I learned enough to know I was horribly sinful and evil, and that I was headed for hell. I also learned I would have to pay dearly for my sins.

I asked Jesus to be my Savior at the age of nine and, at their urging, was baptized and then I was given a list of commandments to follow with warnings of dire consequences for breaking any of those laws. I memorized them and lived in fear of them even as I broke them daily growing up in less than desirable circumstances. Many times, breaking those very commandments was the only thing which kept my siblings and me safe. I was especially guilty of not honoring my parents, which I was reminded continually by a drunken mother; was the most important commandment of all.

Sadly, the Browns, like many spiritual leaders even today, preached a grace for salvation message which was then followed by the laws we must follow to stay saved, which of course was very confusing to me. Deuteronomy 28:1–24, and scriptures like it, were generally the weekly sermon material. Pastor Brown preached Old Testament law, which requires us to do something in order to earn our own blessings and then expects us to do other things in order to escape the many curses which would devour us if we weren't good little boys and girls.

Since I was not taught the Grace of God as a child, Scriptures such as the following, especially being bellowed from the pulpit, scared me half to death and definitely made me want to behave in order to earn my blessings.

> And if you faithfully obey the voice of the Lord your God, being careful to do all His commandments that I command you today, the Lord your God will set you high above all the nations of the earth. And all these blessings shall come upon you and overtake you, if you obey the voice of the Lord your God. Blessed shall you be in the city, and

blessed shall you be in the field. Blessed shall be the fruit of your womb and the fruit of your ground and the fruit of your cattle, the increase of your herds and the young of your flock. Blessed shall be your basket and your kneading bowl. Blessed shall you be when you come in and blessed shall you be when you go out.

The Lord will cause your enemies who rise against you to be defeated before you. They shall come out against you one way and flee before you seven ways. The Lord will command the blessing on you in your barns and in all that you undertake. And He will bless you in the land that the Lord your God is giving you. The Lord will establish you as a people holy to Himself, as He has sworn to you, if you keep the commandments of the Lord your God and walk in His ways. And all the peoples of the earth shall see that you are called by the name of the Lord, and they shall be afraid of you. And the Lord will make you abound in prosperity, in the fruit of your womb and in the fruit of your livestock and in the fruit of your ground, within the land that the Lord swore to your fathers to give you. The Lord will open to you His good treasury, the heavens, to give the rain to your land in its season and to bless all the work of your hands. And you shall lend too many nations, but you shall not borrow. And the Lord will make you the head and not the tail, and you shall only go up and not down, if you obey the commandments of the Lord your God, which I command you today, being careful to do them, and if you do not turn aside from any of the words that I command you today, to the right hand or to the left, to go after other gods to serve them.

But if you will not obey the voice of the Lord your God or be careful to do all His commandments and His statutes that I command you today, then all these curses shall come upon you and overtake you. Cursed shall you be in the city, and cursed shall you be in the field. Cursed shall be your basket and your kneading bowl. Cursed shall be the fruit of your womb and the fruit of your ground, the increase of your herds and the young of your flock. Cursed shall you be when you come in, and cursed shall you be when you go out.

The Lord will send on you curses, confusion, and frustration in all that you undertake to do, until you are destroyed and perish quickly on account of the evil of your deeds, because you have forsaken me. The Lord will make the pestilence stick to you until He has consumed you off the land that you are entering to take possession of it. The Lord will strike you with wasting disease and with fever, inflammation and fiery heat, and with drought and with blight and with mildew. They shall pursue you until you perish. And the heavens over your head shall be bronze, and the earth under you shall be iron. The Lord will make the rain of your land powder. From heaven dust shall come down on you until you are destroyed. (Deut. 28:1–24, ESV)

Whew, right? Believe me when I tell you that I didn't want to get on the wrong side of Scripture like that, but I was a kid, a broken, wounded, imperfect kid who grew up to be a very broken, wounded, imperfect adult.

Ironic the things we do to those we care for, supposedly in the name of God. Many of us have been indoctrinated into a religion of fear and thinking of God as a big mean guy in the sky with a stick, who is ready to knock us down if we make a mistake. When we speak of a loving God who accepts us as His children when we trust in and believe on Jesus and then punishes us with a threat of hell when we mess up, ultimately confusion prevails, especially among our children. No wonder then that countless young people don't want anything to do with the angry condemning God introduced to them in various churches and homes around the world today.

I asked Jesus to be my Savior and made my confession in front of the whole congregation of Pastor Brown's church. I was baptized along with several others including my sister Robin. I tried really hard for years to be saved! To stay saved; to be good enough to deserve His love. I believe looking back that I did that as much for Pastor Brown, as I did for me.

I didn't really believe God loved me. How could He? No one else did. After all the things which had been done to me, I was dirty and used. Besides, if He loved me so much, why didn't He save me all the times I cried out in terror? I was sure that I was so bad, so guilty, and so deserving of His anger that I spent the following forty-seven years of my life, following my baptism and up to my cancer diagnosis, believing to some degree that He hated me, or had deserted me. And I convinced myself that I didn't really care. I could do it myself. I'd always done it myself. I didn't need Him or anyone else.

Oh, I pretended pretty well. And, after marrying a pastor, I pretended even better. On Sundays, I sang and prayed out loud "praising the Lord." I owned a Bible which had just about all the scriptures highlighted in every color possible. I volunteered all over town and visited the sick and imprisoned; I took food to shut-ins and taught Sunday school and vacation Bible school all in an effort to help God see how deserving I was of a place in heaven. Then, on Sundays, my husband and I would argue and yell at each other all the way to church, "get along" for a couple of hours while we were in the spotlight and argue all the way back home again. I would strive like crazy all week to be good enough, and then every time I messed up, which happened pretty regularly, I figured I had to begin all over again. How could I ever be sure?

My husband was the first person in my life who'd ever told me I didn't have to be good enough for God to love me because that's why Jesus died, but he'd been beat down horribly as a child just as I had, and at that particular time in his life, deep down inside, he didn't really believe all that unconditional grace stuff anymore than I did.

We'd both been married before, a big no-no in many religious denominations. He'd been married to a woman who'd cheated with another man and then refused to attend counseling with him to restore their life together; and I'd been married to two different men who'd cheated numerous times, beat me brutally, gambled, drank, used drugs, and were all around not very nice people (I could really pick them back then).

Done with men and marriage after the second divorce, I'd decided I wasn't very good at it and didn't see any reason to put my children through more pain than they'd already endured during those previous eighteen years. My mother was married five times, and like it or not, I seemed to be following in her footsteps, so I would put a stop to it now.

I'd lost a child too, a little baby boy when he was only eight months old, and I was still very angry at God for that, though I was sure in some way it was payback for some of the evils of my life, and I knew I probably deserved it.

Church service on a regular basis was something I'd not done as a child, except for that brief period with the Browns, and when I began to attend as an adult, I know my motivations were wrong to a certain degree. I wanted to know more of God and why He'd let the world beat me down so hard, but I didn't know how to know Him better, and I certainly wasn't choosing churches that were helping me to attain that goal.

Still sure, at that time, on some level that I earned brownie points each time I sat my butt in a church pew or helped out with VBS or cleaning the sanctuary, I tried with all my might to be holy in the eyes of anyone who might be watching. I didn't feel very holy though. I did want my children to know Jesus, but they were being indoctrinated into the same bog of death that held me hostage most of my life. I just didn't know what to do about it.

My life had been filled with years of pain and sorrow, and I simply didn't know that He could, or even wanted to, heal me of the darkness and hurt of my past. Little did I know, at that time, He loved me so much He wanted to give me beauty for ashes and return to me double for my former trouble. No one ever shared with me before that God truly loved me, that He desired to help me and that I only had to ask.

> Instead of your shame there shall be a double portion; instead of dishonor they shall rejoice in their lot; therefore in their land they shall possess a double portion; they shall have everlasting joy. (Isa. 61:7, ESV)

Let's face it. Everyone has stories. Some are more tragic than others, but each one leaves a fond memory or a scar. I once heard that our scars show where we've been, but they don't determine where we're going. I praise God that once we give our lives completely over to the Lord, He orders our steps and he heals those wounds little by little. And, if we allow Him to, He will fill our hearts with His peace.

> So also you have sorrow now, but I will see you again and your hearts will rejoice, and no one will take your joy from you. In that day you will ask nothing of me. Truly, truly I say to you, whatever you ask of the Father in my name, He will give it to you. Until now you have asked nothing in my name. Ask and you will receive, that your joy may be full. (John 16:22–24, esv)

When I met Marty, I have to admit I was a very strong, stubborn, independent woman, and had come to the conclusion I didn't need anyone in my life, especially a man, and most certainly not some faraway spirit in the sky. No one had ever taken care of me or protected me, as far as I was concerned, not even God. I could do it myself! I'd proven to myself on many occasions in personal and business situations that I was as self sufficient as anyone. Marty pursued and eventually won me over though

I'm sure he wondered many times after what he had gotten himself into, or if I was worth it.

Honestly, I don't know how my husband handled being married to me those first years. Defiant and argumentative, I sincerely thought I was always right. I know I made his life almost unbearable for quite some time. God must have given him a gift of patience unheard of before in all of history. I would not give in, simply was not going to allow myself to be vulnerable. Tired of being hurt by every person who came into my life, I refused to open up and share myself with anyone. It took years for my patient husband to tear down the walls I'd built, and he did it with kindness and compassion.

Throughout those years, when things didn't go my way, it made me angry because I felt my power was tied up in how much control I had over the people and situations in my life. When I finally came into the knowledge that God is my only source and strength, I calmed down quite a bit. At last, I came to understand that when I resorted to anger and lashed out all I was doing was handing my power over to whomever or whatever was troubling me.

My life changed when I trusted Jesus. I learned that through Him, I had the power to control my actions and emotions, and those were the only things I needed to control. I could turn the rest of it over to Him. From that point forward, He would fight my battles for me. What a wonderful Savior!

I would never have admitted any of these things even five years ago. Facing the truth about ourselves can be a very painful thing. I wish I'd come to the realization of these truths long before I did, as my children's lives could have been much easier than they were, but my wise daughter has informed me that they are the people they are today because of the things they endured as children, and I like the people they are today, so I am thankful God was able to do something positive in their young lives in spite of my mistakes and misjudgments.

Our years of being pastors taught me very little about anything except the politics of churches. Oh, I loved and cared for the people in our charge, especially the children, but I continued to be the bossy, in charge, hard-to-live-with person I'd been for years; funny how sitting in a church doesn't automatically make us compassionate and Christlike. I read my Bible diligently, studied to show myself approved and was licensed in the denomination where my husband was pastor. *I was very, very proud of myself.*

You might think that working with children and teaching the Word would soften me, give me a better perspective, you know all of that Bible reading and everything. But, because I was still living under the law and the condemnation that accompanies that law, my eyes only saw the "must dos" and "must not dos" written in those Scriptures. I saw law and more rules to follow, for myself, for our own children, and for the teenagers I was teaching.

Looking back on those years of ministering, I know I truly believed, at least at that time, I had a duty to teach our children and those in my Sunday school classes the same things which were beat into my head for so many years. I didn't know any better then and was convinced when I didn't feel forgiven that I just wasn't being hard enough on myself or on those young people. I wanted to do the right thing, but didn't know yet what the right thing was. I quietly beat myself up day after day, but the longer I studied the wrong message, the more buried in the death of law I became. I know now how wrong I was, but until we came into possession of this wonderful grace message, I was sure we were doing the right thing, and I was sure I had all the right answers, as I'm sure many others do.

> For by the grace given to me I say to everyone among you not to think of himself more highly than he ought to think, but to think with sober judgment, each according to the measure of faith that God has assigned. (Rom. 12:3, ESV)

I hadn't learned to live in harmony with anyone, least of all my husband.

> Live in harmony with one another. Do not be haughty, but associate with the lowly. Never be wise in your own sight. Repay no one evil for evil, but give thought to do what is honorable in the sight of all. If possible so far as it depends on you, live peaceably with all. (Rom. 12:16–18, ESV)

I for one now believe that until our eyes and ears are opened through hearts which yearn for Christ, we can't clearly see the grace that is staring us right in the face. Until the scales of self righteousness and self dependence fall from our eyes, we will not see that the price has already been paid, and Jesus is the one who has paid that price. He has done the work for us and no amount of self effort will achieve those things set aside for the Holy Spirit.

> Then turning to the disciples He said privately, "Blessed are the eyes that see what you see! For I tell you that many prophets and kings desired to see what you see, and did not see it, and to hear what you hear, and did not hear it." (Luke:10:23–24, ESV)
>
> For this people's heart has grown dull, and with their ears they can barely hear, and their eyes they have closed; lest they should see with their eyes and hear with their ears and understand with their heart and turn, and I would heal them. (Acts: 28:27, ESV)

Though we saw the ministry growing even in the midst of our folly and many people were saved on a regular basis, we knew something was wrong; where was the joy that was supposed to fill us? The whole thing felt more like a job than a joy. We were working so very hard trying to be holy, to pay for our past sins by being good enough so that maybe He wouldn't remember who we'd been, but see us for the works we were performing. We didn't know then that once we'd asked Him into our hearts, He didn't remember our sins anymore, and when He looked at us, He saw only His dear Son.

> For He finds fault with them when He says: "Behold, the days are coming, declares the Lord, when I will establish a new covenant with the house of Israel and with the house of Judah, not like the covenant that I made with their fathers on the day when I took them by the hand to bring them out of the land of Egypt. For they did not continue in my covenant, and so I showed no concern for them, declares the Lord. For this is the covenant that I will make with the house of Israel after those days, declares the Lord: I will put my laws into their minds, and write them on their hearts, and I will be their God,

and they shall be my people. And they shall not teach, each one his neighbor and each one his brother, saying, 'Know the Lord', for they shall all know me, from the least of them to the greatest. For I will be merciful toward their iniquities, and I will remember their sins no more." (Heb. 8:8–12, ESV)

WHAT OF CHRIST?

When Marty and I initially began to study more of the radical grace message in June of 2010, we were at first racked with guilt bordering on feelings of heresy or blasphemy. We didn't know what to think. Pouring over Scripture, we could see that every bit of what we were reading made sense, but it was so different from anything either of us had been taught in regard to spiritual beliefs, we were puzzled and frightened. It's hard to unlearn everything that's been shoved down your throat your whole life.

Having been schooled on a mixture of Old Testament law and New Testament grace combined as truth, we were confused, but not only having been taught, now having been the teachers to so many for decades, we were torn. Was the truth as we'd known it for so long not the actual truth? Had we been preaching lies to the very people we held dear, the children whose spiritual growth was entrusted to us?

The Word says that the law was given through Moses and that Truth and Grace came through Jesus Christ, so clearly the law is not truth for the believer.

> For the Law was given through Moses; Grace and Truth came through Jesus Christ (John 1:17, ESV).

We know the Bible admonishes us to study to show ourselves approved and so we did.

> Do your best to present yourself to God as one approved, a worker who has no need to be ashamed, rightly handling the Word of Truth (2 Tim. 2:15, ESV).

We began to dissect the Scriptures, going back to original Greek and Hebrew texts, and we became more convinced we had believed in error previously;

and we grew more comfortable with this Gospel of grace and love. We discovered that the only true Gospel is the grace of Christ and His sacrifice. Anything else is a deception of man and Satan to keep people in the dark about how to have complete victory in Christ.

I was so glad we'd begun to study before my diagnosis, as I was much more accepting of a message that tells me He already paid for my healing when I was frightened and I so desperately needed that specific communication.

So much of my previous attitude about God had been in seeing an entity that was faraway and unreachable. A God who had the ability to heal and might even heal others, but certainly not me; but I was beginning to see into the mind of a God who created me and loved me unconditionally; a Lord who was willing to die for me and rise again so that by believing in Him I might become the righteousness of God in Christ through Him.

> For our sake He made Him to be sin who knew no sin, so that in Him we might become the righteousness of God (2 Cor 5:21, ESV).

I was, at last, learning to value myself through His eyes and realize that I serve a Redeemer who is not only able to do all He has promised, but who is absolutely willing. He wants to know me, and He wants me to know Him. At long last, I could genuinely learn to pray. Never again would my prayers be wooden and phony. Never again would I feel the need to impress the creator who knew me inside and out; the one who knows what I will ask before I could ever ask Him.

What a joy to serve a God who hears my needs and is waiting eagerly to help. My prayers became more than mere words, but instead an attitude which would see me through each day. *Jesus became my best friend, my confidant, my abundant provider.*

> Now to Him who is able to do far more abundantly than all that we ask or think according to the power at work within us, to Him be glory in the church and in Christ Jesus throughout all generations, forever and ever. Amen. (Eph. 3:20–21, ESV)

A MATTER OF FAITH

For a year and a half, we waited. I'd been told at the beginning of my cancer journey the disease was too far advanced for any conventional chemotherapy treatments, which were available at that time. The cancer had been caught much too late and had metastasized to so many different locations in my torso, the doctor said, that the amount of chemo needed to treat me would most likely kill me and would only be considered as a last resort.

Radiation was also not a viable option for me at that time, as there were too many affected sites, and radiation is a localized treatment. Instead, I was offered a new test drug, which was being studied for cancers such as the one I was dealing with. This test drug was not touted as a cure; we were told it couldn't rid me of the disease, but might delay the inevitable, or even cause the disease to be chronic, versus terminal, at least until it stopped working.

Causing me to experience severe, daily migraine headaches the treatment had me spending a great deal of time in quiet, darkened rooms, but I didn't give up hope. Equally difficult was the arthritis in my hands, knees, and hips, which was a common side effect and worsened with each passing day, so movement was very painful, and my writing was almost completely abandoned for some time.

I learned a great deal about dependence on God during this time. I'd never been one to ask for help (being a firm believer since childhood that I can do it myself), or even to accept assistance from friends or family when they offered, but my family and friends became my lifeline throughout this time. I even came to know that God had good plans for me.

> For I know the plans I have for you, declares the Lord, plans for your welfare and not for evil, to give you a future and a hope. Then you

will call upon me and come and pray to me,
and I will hear you." (Jer. 29:11–12, ESV)

I turned to the Lord every day in prayer and grew
to know little by little, more and more that He is my
refuge, my strength and that He truly does love me.

> God is our refuge and strength, a very present
> help in trouble (Ps. 46:1, ESV).

As He became my best friend and the one I could
depend on, my attitude toward the rest of the world,
including toward my husband, began to change. I
finally started believing God for everything I would
need for my well-being, my emotional stability, and
even my financial needs.

> And we know that for those who love God
> all things work together for good, for those
> who are called according to His purpose
> (Rom. 8:28, ESV).

> And my God will supply every need of yours
> according to His riches in glory in Christ
> Jesus (Phil. 4:19, ESV).

It was during this time that some of my doctors and I had a running debate about the Lord. There was a certain doctor, who, when I would tell him that I knew I was already healed, not going to be healed in the future, but already healed, would remind me of what the new PET scans and CAT scans showed. But, I was determined not to let my circumstances rule the day, and to completely lean on the promises of God. To his credit he would pray with me during each visit, hug me, and wish me luck in my journey. He retired shortly after my initial diagnoses and I was reassigned to another doctor.

> "Sanctify them in the truth; your Word is truth" (John 17:17, ESV).

I was finally beginning to learn and at last I knew I would not be swayed ever again by the words of mere men.

> No distrust made him waver concerning the promise of God, but he grew strong in his faith as he gave glory to God fully convinced that God was able to do what He had promised. (Rom. 4 20–21, ESV)

> Let us hold fast the confession of our hope without wavering, for He who promised is faithful. (Heb. 10:23, ESV)

And now I knew without a doubt that God had promised me not only healing, but eternal life in Him!

> And this is the promise that He made to us—eternal life (1 John 2:25, ESV).

As time passed, I was seeing myself as God's beloved child; and the more I imagined myself as His child, the more confident I became in the healing I believed had already been accomplished. As that confidence in Him grew and the knowledge of my healing solidified in my heart, the less I lived in the fear, which had once engulfed me. I was once and for all embracing the truth He meant for me to see. I began to see myself as His child, and the conqueror His Word tells me I am! I am finally free!

> For you did not receive the spirit of slavery to fall back into fear, but you have received the spirit of adoption as sons, by whom we cry, Abba! Father! The Spirit Himself bears

witness with our spirit that we are children of God, and if children, then heirs-heirs of God and fellow heirs with Christ, provided we suffer with Him in order that we may also be glorified with Him. (Rom. 8:15–17, ESV)

No in all these things we are more than conquerors through Him who loved us. For I am sure that neither death nor life, nor angels nor rulers, nor things present nor things to come, nor powers, nor height nor depth, nor anything else in all creation, will be able to separate us from the love of God in Christ Jesus our Lord. (Rom. 8:37–39, ESV)

And you will know the truth and the truth will make you free. (John 8:32, ESV)

I eventually began to smile and laugh a little. Growing up in the circumstances of my youth and with the number of responsibilities I'd shouldered as a child, I'd become quite a serious and somber adult. Very dependable and hardworking, though both honorable traits, I'd never learned to enjoy my life or have fun. My poor husband had been trying to make me laugh for years with silly jokes and goofy voices, and our children actually made fun of me, telling me I must be FBI.

We'd watched a movie when they were young, *Men in Black*, in which the character played by Tommy Lee Jones is an FBI agent. In one scene, that FBI agent announces who they are to a woman they've come to question. The woman says to the FBI agent, "Are you here to make fun of me too?" and the FBI agent answers, "No, ma'am. We at the FBI have no sense of humor that we're aware of." This line became a family joke about my need to find logic in even the funniest of situations.

I desperately wanted to be a person my husband and children would like and want to be around, but up to that point in time, I'd always seemed to revert to analyzing every state of affairs to see how I could take care of things by myself and find a sense of reason. I persistently insisted everything must work out in a way, which could make sense. I couldn't seem to be at ease in any circumstance in which I wasn't in control, and laughter was an uncontrollable action with too many variables. I'm happy to report I laugh more now, and though God has had to work very hard with me, I am not quite so serious anymore.

Miracles

After eighteen months of treatments, prayer, and people from every quarter who were hesitant to believe my claim of healing, you might think I would give up. But I believe I mentioned I was stubborn. My husband Marty, our daughter Liz, and I prayed and took communion every day, with even more confidence once we began to fully understand the importance of the act of deliverance, which was finished on the cross at Calvary. We thanked God for my healing daily, even when there was not yet any evidence of that healing.

Many were used to my claims of healing and wholeness, even when the scans showed otherwise, and they simply shook their heads in, what seemed like, collective annoyance.

I'd started to share the Word with other patients and even some nurses and doctors during my long hours at the cancer center, and as my confidence grew in the grace message, which was certainly saving my life, I grew bolder in my evangelism. Passing out Bibles and other books of encouragement, I saw many new friends trust Jesus as Savior and become brothers and sisters in Christ. I also baked and brought gifts to the cancer center to share with the employees there and all those new friends.

Coming to understand God was using the disease many would consider evil, and that I once thought a chastisement, to reach others and bring into the kingdom many new believers, I threw myself into my new role of evangelist with enthusiasm. I'd come to believe this cancer was not a punishment from God, but the consequence of living in a fallen world; a tool which Satan used trying to cause me to lose faith in my creator; and now a tool which God was using to reach others who might never hear of Him any other way. What a blessing.

Then, a year and a half after first diagnosis, my doctor saw evidence of my disease shrinking. The test drug I was taking was not a cure, I had been told that emphatically, but here we were seeing definite changes. I told him I believed it was the beginning of the physical manifestation of healing I knew had already taken place. I went home and shared the news with my family and we rejoiced.

Deciding to watch me closely and do another scan in six weeks, my oncologist approached the news with a wait and see attitude. Results of the new scan showed more change and healing, which should not necessarily have been occurring on my current treatment. My doctor seemed puzzled at the changes, but I was even more hopeful. I knew God was working my miracle. The doctor scheduled another test for six weeks hence. I told him I knew when I came back in six weeks the cancer would be gone. Again, I went home and shared the news with my family, and again, we celebrated because we knew God was in the process of showing the world something miraculous through me.

This time though, I knew it didn't have anything to do with my worth or lack of it. I knew it didn't have anything to do with the merit of my husband's prayers. I knew I hadn't done anything to cause me to be the recipient of this miracle. God healed me (not that He was going to heal me, but that He had already healed me) because He is good; because He loves me and because Jesus already paid the price for my healing. Praise God!

At church that week, a pastor friend said, "But what are you going to do if you aren't healed when you go back in six weeks? Will that make you lose faith in God?" I replied, "That would imply that I am not already healed. I trust God for His promises, and by His stripes, I am healed." I determined my confession could no longer be one of sickness, lack, fear, and weakness but one of healing, provision, safety in Christ, and strength in His love. I am no longer Satan's captive, but God's redeemed. I am truly safe in the Father's hand.

> I give them eternal life, and they will never perish, and no one will snatch them out of my hand. My Father, who has given them to

me, is greater than all, and no one is able to snatch them out of the Father's hand. (John 10:28–29, ESV)

I returned in six weeks for my scheduled PET scan on a Monday. The following Wednesday, I received a call from the nurse asking me if I could come down to the center to see the doctor. I told her I had an appointment on Friday, and she insisted the doctor wanted to see me now. I became excited and said to her. "They're gone, aren't they? I knew it!"

She returned with, "Donna, you know I can't tell you about it over the phone. Just get down here."

When I was ushered into the doc's office, the nurse smiled at me, and I was reassured that the news was good. When my physician entered, the first words out of his mouth were, "Okay, Mrs. Smarty Pants, you've got your miracle. The tumors are gone. I can't explain it, but they're gone."

I couldn't wait to call my husband and kids; and then to call all the relatives, pastors, friends, and neighbors who'd been including me in their prayers for a year and a half, even if they'd thought I was crazy for most of it.

I was still on the 1 test drug with its crazy side effects, and the migraine headaches were getting worse all the time, but I was confident God had a plan for that too.

Pretty soon, I was getting phone calls from pastor friends and other churches asking me to come give my testimony, and I was thrilled to share my story with others if it would give them the hope to overcome their own circumstances with God's help.

GO TELL IT ON THE MOUNTAIN

My testimony in churches we visited brought hope to many and elicited some rather strange responses from others. I discovered little by little that God must meet each person where they are and work through their specific issues with them just as He had done with me. When I'd first begun to share the news of Jesus and then later my testimony of God healing me, mind, body, and spirit, I truly believed if I were going to share the Gospel, it must also be my responsibility to make sure the person I was sharing with received that message and believed.

I was devastated when some would hesitate, or worse, tell me they weren't interested in receiving the free gift Jesus provided. I eventually learned that it is my duty as a Christian to share the Gospel, but not my function to make people believe. Belief must be a personal choice.

I added new people to my prayer list every day and continued to share. I learned through trial and error that God would provide someone in that person's life who would carry on the attempt to win them over until either the job was done, or they refused His love entirely.

> I planted, Apollos watered, but God gave the growth. So neither he who plants nor he who waters is anything, but only God who gives the growth (1 Cor. 3:6–7, ESV).

I didn't want to see anyone lost, and it broke my heart when some turned their backs on Him, but we each have a selection to make, and God is a gentleman, He doesn't want to be forced down anyone's throat. When I share the Lord and someone comes to know Him, it is not my glory but His. And, if it is His glory, then it is He that will work in their hearts to bring them around. God, even more than I, does not want to see anyone lost. Again, prayer was the answer.

The Lord is not slow to fulfill His promise as some count slowness, but is patient toward you, not wishing that any should perish, but that all should reach repentance (2 Pet. 3:9, ESV).

On one occasion where I was asked to give my testimony in a local church setting, my husband and I were involved later in a small group study where people there were encouraged to ask questions. A young man wanted to know what I thought was so special about me that God would save me and not his mother, who had apparently died some months earlier. He was very angry. I told him I didn't have the answer to that question, only that I knew it didn't have anything to do with me or anyone being more special than anyone else. After all, God loves every one of His children equally.

Other than the fact that I'd come to know my healing already took place two thousand years ago and we serve a loving God, I am only a human being, and I don't have all the answers. I do know though that His healing, which is already accomplished, is available to all who believe. He then remarked, "You didn't answer my question. Why you and not my mother?" It was fruitless at that point to try to answer without first giving him a full understanding of true grace.

In his current state of anger, I didn't think he was ready to receive anything from me. He felt somehow that I was telling people I deserved the healing I received when that assumption could not be further from the truth. The attacks continued.

At the same meeting, a woman told me how she alone deserved God's best because she had been an elder of the church for so long, and it made her angry to see someone else receive a blessing she knew was designated for her. I'm happy to tell you there were others who thanked me for sharing my story and wished me future good health, but there were some who felt as though my receipt of a blessing somehow meant there would be fewer blessings to go around and that might mean they would miss out on theirs.

My husband and I spent most of that evening and several others expounding on a supernatural, loving God, who is the creator of the universe. We were attempting to describe a God who doesn't run out of love no matter how much He gives away to a room full of people who saw Him exactly the way I did before I'd come to know Him better, and it was a challenge indeed. I was confident they could all know the same magnificent, powerful God I knew if they would only give themselves a chance through trusting Him, study, and prayer.

I knew, however, the length of time it had taken for the Lord to begin getting through to me, so it helped me to be patient with those who were still putting limits on Him and His infinite love. I also knew God was using us for His purpose, but I quit thinking at that point it was up to me too have all the answers. I came to realize God would fill our mouths with the words we needed as the time came for us to use them.

Marty and I prayed every day for the words to say and the understanding of when to say them to people we met along the way, and we had many wonderful opportunities in our day-to-day experiences to give our testimony and pray for those who decided to trust Jesus or who finally believed for healing.

Oddly, one of the things I heard most from people in our church when we acted as their spiritual leaders or from others at meetings where we were giving testimony was, "But I can tell you are such a good person. You deserved to be healed." For me, that was the strangest comment of all. I had to tell folks since they didn't live with me that they had no idea what my family put up with for many years, or indeed what they still endured now and that if they really knew me they would understand that I above all did not deserve healing, but that was secondary.

Again, whether we were speaking to people who didn't think they were good enough, as we had personally felt for so many years; or people who thought a family member or friend of theirs was better than we were and deserved the healing I'd received, the message had to be delivered that our righteousness is as filthy rags in His sight (Isa. 64:6). He is the only one righteous indeed, and we are merely righteous in Him. My healing had *nothing* to do with me, or my being worthy, praise God and yours has *nothing* to do with you!

My Grace Is Sufficient

For another year and a half after the miraculous disappearance of my cancer, I continued to have severe arthritis and migraines due to those test drugs I was receiving. My oncologist didn't want to take me off the medication since he was sure it was the sole reason I was currently in remission. We prayed and thanked God every day for relief from the headaches, as if it was already accomplished, and waited for the physical manifestation of the healing from those often debilitating migraines. My physician tried several different pain medications and treatments, all of which caused me vicious nausea, and he eventually sent me in for Botox injections into my head, but nothing helped.

We refused to stop believing though. By this time, we'd learned over and over that God will use every situation in our lives for good because He loves us. We knew He was going to do something which would spread the Gospel and minister to many in new places, places I wouldn't have thought to go on my own. I no longer functioned from fear, but trusted wholly in Him. Finally realizing God is good all the time!

In July of 2013, I felt a small lump in my left upper chest. I knew right away what it was, and I told my doctor about it when I went in for my regular checkup, but he dismissed it and told me it was near my port and was probably just some swelling.

The lump grew larger, and in August, while I was seeing a different physician at the center, I pointed it out to him. He also told me he believed it was nothing and dismissed my concerns. "Sometimes, when you've dealt with cancer in the past, every little thing becomes cancer," he told me. This one was smaller, but I was convinced this lump felt the same as the tumor which had begun my whole cancer journey almost three years before—hard and fixed—and I tried very hard to get him to take my situation seriously. Ignored again, I went home to await my next appointment.

September rolled around and the lump had gotten so large it was visibly protruding from my chest, so I asked to see female CPA who I knew was in practice there at the center. She examined me and seemed genuinely concerned. It was a Friday and she ordered a CAT scan, discovering through the test that I had a new tumor in my left chest wall. Further examination proved it was malignant and consisted of the same type of cancer cells which attacked me previously. Surgery was scheduled for that Monday, September 18. I prayed, thanking God for all He's done for me and for the miracles I knew He'd already performed concerning this new challenge.

Interestingly, this time, I wasn't frightened. I knew I could trust the Lord to see me through, and I marveled at the work He'd done in me to get me to this point of absolute confidence. My husband

and daughter were also very calm, and Dave's first sergeant sent him home to be with me for the surgery and recovery after. Compared to the panic-filled bunch from three years earlier, we were completely different creatures, and we all praised God for the work He'd done in us. There's an old saying which goes, "Trouble is inevitable, but misery is optional." We'd learned to accept that in this life, there will be troubles, but if we are trusting Christ, we can avoid the misery, which seems to encapsulate the minds of the rest of the world.

We knew this time what God was capable of, as we had seen His handiwork in our lives before. Of course, His abilities hadn't changed, but gratefully our confidence was sure. We thanked Him for the miracles He would perform through this latest trial—whatever they might be—and we chose to pray and trust Him with our whole hearts.

My surgeon spent quite some time trying to remove all the fingers and tentacles, which the tumor sent weaving throughout the muscles in my chest, but reported to me afterward he was sorry he couldn't get it all. "If only this had been caught a couple of months earlier," he said. "I probably could have contained it all. We won't know if it has spread until the center has a chance to do some new scans."

Again, we prayed. It's difficult to convey the peace and comfort that comes from the simple act of praying, of an uncomplicated talk with our Heavenly Father, but even with the doctor's last words hanging over my head, I could not be swayed. Satan had lost his hold on me for good. Never again would I be tempted to fall back into that pit of despair where I'd wallowed for so long.

In the meantime, I was taken off the cancer drug, which had been causing my migraines and arthritis, since obviously it had stopped working against the cancer, and within ten days, my headaches disappeared completely, and the swelling in my hands began to dissipate. Praise God! He sees the bigger picture and knows what we ultimately need. I was so relieved. An event which to some might seem like a devastating relapse was instead a path to healing.

I felt like a new woman now that I could walk into a bright room without wincing. God is good all the time, and sometimes, He answers prayers in ways we didn't see coming. Now instead of dreading what might be around the corner, I felt eager to see how God would use this latest bit of news for His glory and I was anxious to see what He had in store for us next.

After a long talk with the center's head radiologist, we agreed to do a thirty-three-day round of radiation on my chest, shoulder, neck, and back before we would do our next PET scans. Where for my first cancer diagnosis radiation wasn't an option, now we were looking at keeping a single tumor location from spreading, and he thought this course of action represented my best option. "Breast cancer tends to head for the brain," he said, "and we'd better contain it before this goes any further." Again, we prayed and felt genuinely assured. We knew God had a plan and that His plans for us are for good and not for evil.

I said before that I don't believe God causes bad things to happen to us, or even that He just watches us flounder when they do. I do know now that He allows things which the world might consider evil to come into our lives. After all, everything passes through His hands, but He allows those things for a purpose, and when looking at the bigger picture, those things, which to us may appear evil, are actually the course to a greater good.

For instance, you or I might consider a thing or circumstance wicked, but is it necessarily malevolence in the larger scheme? If that thing or circumstance creates the very path that causes us to come to know the Lord, or repairs relationships we've allowed to go by the wayside, how can it be considered evil? I believe He uses everything that the world, or Satan, throws at us and turns those things around to use them for good, to bring more people to Him.

> As for you, you meant evil against me, but God meant it for good, to bring it about that many people should be kept alive, as they are today (Gen. 50:20, ESV).

For thirty-three days, my husband and I passed out Bibles and ministered to people in the radiology waiting room, as I waited each day for radiation treatment. This was actually a room I'd never entered in my three previous years of treatment at the cancer center. A space I probably never would have entered, as it was in a completely different wing of the center, if I hadn't needed those treatments.

We made lots of new friends and prayed with many of those friends as they came to trust Jesus as Lord and Savior. God works in mysterious ways to achieve the things which will bring more people to the knowledge of His grace. I'm learning as I open my life to be used of Him that no matter the circumstances, He graciously steps in with His peace and love to reach many. God is so good!

Trusting Him

In November of 2013, the cancer center techs performed PET scans, and when I met with my doctor a few days later, she told me the cancer had sadly spread to my left lung. Upset that it had gotten so far, she was angry that the other doctors ignored my instincts, and we both agreed if it had been caught when I'd first found the lump, it likely could have been halted in its tracks, but what was done was done.

My attitude is different this time around. I know God loves me, not because I deserve it or have done anything to earn it, but because He is Love. I know I am favored because He loves me; and I know that I am the righteousness of God in Christ, not for anything I have accomplished, but because of the sacrifice Jesus made for me.

> For our sake He made him to be sin who knew no sin, so that in Him we might become the righteousness of God (2 Cor. 5:21, ESV).

This time, I have come from a place of experience. I know I've seen His miracles at work in my life and in the lives of others. I am born again to a living hope. Though trials have come into my life; this time my confidence is sure. This time I have no doubt.

Since that November examination, which showed three new tumors in my left lung, a new scan was done in April of 2015, and praise God, one of the tumors is gone and a second has gone dark. Though there is a new spot on my breast bone, I'm sure He has plans for that too! He is at work again freeing me from satin's snares!

> Blessed be the God and Father of our Lord Jesus Christ! According to His great mercy, He has caused us to be born again to a living hope through the resurrection of Jesus Christ from the dead, to an inheritance that is

imperishable, undefiled, and unfading, kept in heaven for you, who by God's power are being guarded through faith for a salvation ready to be revealed in the last time. In this you rejoice, though now for a little while, if necessary, you have been grieved by various trials, so that the tested genuineness of your faith-more precious than gold that perishes though it is tested by fire-may be found to result in praise and glory and honor at the revelation of Jesus Christ. Though you have not seen Him, you love Him. Though you do not now see Him, you believe in Him and rejoice with joy that is inexpressible and filled with glory, obtaining the outcome of your faith, the salvation of your souls. (1 Pet. 1:3–9, ESV)

In whatever way God has decided to use me I am ready. I know that by His stripes, I was healed over two thousand years ago. Praise the Lord!

He Himself bore our sins in His body on the tree, that we might die to sin and live to righteousness. By His wounds you have been healed (1 Pet. 2:24, ESV).

I am amazed by God's miraculous love and by the way it changes everything! Life used to be so hard, even simple things like household chores and shopping were dreaded events. I was heavy with the burdens of my past and the bother of day to day living. But I have discovered when I take God with me wherever I go, He makes my life ever so much easier. He opens doors and makes crooked places straight.

My load is lighter as I follow Him. In Psalm 23:5–6, David said,

> You prepare a table before me in the presence of my enemies; you anoint my head with oil; my cup overflows. Surely goodness and mercy shall follow me all the days of my life, and I shall dwell in the house of the Lord forever. (ESV)

In speaking with various people and groups over these past five years, a line of questions that repeatedly arise are these: If God is a loving God, why do bad things happen? Why do people get cancer and other diseases? My answer would be simply that we are born into a sinful world. Where there is sin, there is disease and pain; that is the way of it. God is saddened by the sin in which we indulge, but He is a gentleman and will not force Himself on anyone. He offers us redemption through His blood and a way out, but we are a people of choices and whether or not to trust Him is one of the choices we must make.

> In Him we have redemption through His blood, the forgiveness of our trespasses, according to the riches of His grace (Eph. 1:7, ESV).

Those same people will ask why a God who can perform miracles doesn't just do something. My answer to that is, He did do something. He created us! If all people would trust Him, love the way He loves and treat others with that love of Christ, can you imagine how much better a place to live this world would be? It is up to us as His children to make that wish a reality.

He puts people in my path daily—people who don't know Him or who need help in some way. God wants to save us by His grace, to seat us in heavenly places with Christ Jesus, but we must open our lives to His love and realize we are not getting there by our own works. We've been given this miraculous gift of His grace, and it is our honor to share the message of His love and grace with those He places in our lives along the way.

> But God being rich in mercy, because of the great love with which He loved us, even when we were dead in our trespasses, made us alive together with Christ-by grace you have been saved—and raised us up with Him seated us with Him in the heavenly places in Christ Jesus, so that in the coming ages He might show the immeasurable riches of His grace in kindness toward us in Christ Jesus. For by grace you have been saved through faith. And this is not your own doing; it is the gift of God. Not a result of works, so that no one may boast. (Eph. 2:4–9, ESV)

It is up to me to use the power He has given me through the Holy Spirit to make a difference in the lives of the people He places in my path. I am no longer ashamed or embarrassed to ask someone if they know Jesus. I used to feel that sharing my faith in Christ was an imposition to those with whom I was sharing, but I've gotten over that falsehood. Now, I absolutely will not shove Him down their throats, but I will certainly share my testimony and invite them to know Him, with great joy. As a believer, I can share Jesus in many ways; I can visit the elderly or prison inmates; I can feed the hungry, put shoes on the feet of children, offer rides, be a child advocate, give money for missions, offer a word of kindness to brighten someone's day, or pray for someone's health and circumstances. God gives us so many tools to use in winning others to the kingdom, but it is up to us to use them.

Others might say to me, "Why should I share Jesus? Isn't it enough that He is my Savior? I don't want to be one of those pushy Christians. Besides, I'm not God. If He wants it done why doesn't He do it Himself?" Or, "That's why God made ministers. It's their job to evangelize not mine."

I beg to differ with those of that opinion. When we come to know Jesus as our personal Savior, we become His disciples, and as His disciples, we are given "The Great Commission." And let's get real. It isn't called the great suggestion; it's called "The Great Commission" for a reason!

> And Jesus came and said to them, "All authority in heaven and on earth has been given to me. Go therefore and make disciples of all nations, baptizing them in the name of the Father and of the Son and of the Holy Spirit, teaching them to observe all that I have commanded you. And behold, I am with you always, to the end of the age. (Matt.28:18–20, ESV)
>
> And He said to them, "Go into all the world and proclaim the Gospel to the whole creation. Whoever believes and is baptized will be saved, but whoever does not believe will be condemned." (Mark 16:15–16, ESV)

Clearly, God intends for us to be the messengers of His Gospel of peace and grace! I ask many people after statements such as those above, "Why wouldn't you want to share the best thing that ever happened to you, especially with those you love? Why would you want anyone to go to hell if you have the power to give them the information which will save them in Christ?" I tend to wonder how close a person's relationship with the Lord is if they don't want to share Him with others. Do they know the same Jesus I know? If they did, they'd be shouting His Name from the rooftops!

I've even had people ask me, "If God is so loving and caring, why would He condemn anyone to hell?" Well, my answer to that question is that since salvation is a choice we make to trust Jesus, then condemnation is a choice we make not to trust Jesus.

Some people equate sharing Jesus with doing something to earn salvation, but again I disagree! Once we've trusted Jesus for salvation our eternity is assured, but wouldn't we want to see those we meet along the way have that same assurance?

When I peer into the eyes of someone on their deathbed, who has never asked Jesus to come into their heart, and I see the look of panic which emanates from the mind of the unsaved my heart breaks. Marty and I have come to know that panicked look quite well after many years at the bedsides of the dying. Once we share the undeserved grace of Christ with those frightened souls, the panic leaves their eyes and is replaced by peace. I am honored to share the love of Jesus with any who would listen and believe.

I continually hope that sharing my mess might help someone else find their miracle. I believe Satan gets really angry when my worst mistakes in life end up being a road map, which leads another to the answers that might save their life.

A NEW AND BETTER WAY

Prayer is a personal thing, and I am convinced it's the best gift God has given us for communicating with Him. Many people have told me over the years that they don't know how to pray. Some say it's embarrassing even to try. They feel strange and awkward, or they don't know the right words to use. I've been asked, "How do you know what to say when you pray?" And, "How do you know if He's listening?" Well, I can tell you that I used to believe He wasn't listening to me, but now I know if you are His child, He *is*, without question, listening. And, as for what to say, He is your Father, Creator, and your best friend. He is for you, He is on your side, He loves you! Just open your heart and begin.

> We know that God does not listen to sinners, but if anyone is a worshipper of God and does His will, He listens to him (John 9:31, ESV).

This Scripture might make you ask, as it did me when I began studying in earnest, "Well, is He listening to me? I am after all one of the biggest sinners I know. Is it possible to be a sinner and a worshipper at the same time?" To answer this question, I will ask you to begin seeing yourself as God sees you. If you've trusted Jesus as your Lord and Savior, then when God looks at you, He sees His beloved Son. He no longer sees the sinner you were, but the new creature He is creating in you through Christ. So, He doesn't see the sin He has already forgiven and forgotten, He sees only His much-loved child. Learn to forgive yourself and others as you have been forgiven by your Heavenly Father. If you believe, then you are a worshipper of God, and He *is* listening whenever you come to Him in an attitude of prayer!

> And this is the confidence that we have toward Him, that if we ask anything according to His will He hears us. And if we know that He hears us in whatever we ask, we know that we have the requests that we have asked of Him. (1 John 5:14–15, ESV)

We're told many times throughout Scripture to pray, but we shouldn't be praying because we feel obligated to do so. Prayer should be sincere and heartfelt. Jesus prayed as a way to stay connected to the Father and now that we have been adopted as children and joint heirs with Christ, God is our Father too. He wants to hear from us and about us. Yes, yes, He already knows, but when we take the time to connect with Him He sees the genuineness and faith in our hearts. He wants to help. He lives to help. He is always with us.

> Pray without ceasing. (1 Thess. 5:17, ESV)
>
> I desire then that in every place the men should pray, lifting holy hands without anger or quarreling. (1 Tim. 2:8, ESV)
>
> Is anyone among you suffering? Let him pray. Is anyone cheerful? Let him sing praise.

Is anyone among you sick? Let him call for the elders of the church, and let them pray over him, anointing him with oil in the name of the Lord. And the prayer of faith will save the one who is sick, and the Lord will raise him up. And if he has committed sins he will be forgiven. (James 5:13–15, ESV)

Now that all our children are grown and we have been blessed with many grandchildren, Marty and I have discovered the value of staying connected with those who don't live in the same house with us anymore. We are so delighted when one of our kids, or grandkids, takes the time to call or text us. Life can be pretty hectic, but it can also be sad and lonely without those meaningful human connections.

I would have to believe God feels the same way about staying in touch with us. Sure, sure, I know He is all knowing and all seeing, but it's one thing to know how we are doing and another to hear it directly from our lips to His ears through prayer, just as it is one thing for us to know our kids are doing okay out there and entirely another to know that they care enough to reach out to their dad and mom. And just as we enjoy hearing from our children and grandchildren, God takes great delight in hearing from us. He is not just with us, He is in us and therefore involved in every aspect of our lives if we will only open our hearts and let Him all the way in.

And let's face it, prayer is not just a way to stay connected, but a way for us to let God know that we trust Him with every aspect of our lives. You know, even when He allows events to come into our lives, which we might consider difficult, He is not doing so for His benefit. He already knows what we are capable of, what we are made of, and how much we can stand, After all, He created us. He is simply allowing us to see how strong we are in Him through the adversities which come our way. In this way, He is building our confidence for the things which are coming next.

Once we see that we too can be overcomers through Him, we are ready for anything the world or Satan can throw at us! No one grows in the good times or the mountain top experiences. When everything is going well, we don't stretch and learn; we don't lean on Him. It takes the dark times, the valleys, and the tragic events; those things which feel as if they will wipe us out that cause us to turn to God and grow in ways only He knew we could.

> By this you know the Spirit of God; every spirit that confesses that Jesus Christ has come in the flesh is from God, and every spirit that does not confess Jesus is not from God. This is the spirit of the antichrist, which you heard was coming and now is in the world already. Little children, you are from God and have overcome them, for He who is in you is greater than He who is in the world. (1 John 4:2–4, ESV)

Life is filled with ups and downs. God doesn't tell us that if we come to Him through Jesus, our lives will become easy, or that we will no longer have trials and tribulation. In fact, He tells us that, as His followers, we will have tribulation! He does however promise that He will be with us through the trouble. Satan, the culture of mankind and the workings of the world are at conflict with a godly life, but through Jesus's sacrifice, He has overcome the world.

> I have said these things to you, that in me you may have peace. In the world you will have tribulation. But take heart; I have overcome the world (John 16:33, ESV).

Nowhere in Scripture are we told He will remove our problems, but He does tell us He will never leave us or forsake us and that we can count on Him to walk with us through life's problems. All we must do is go to Him in prayer.

> Keep your life free from love of money, and be content with what you have, for He has said, "I will never leave you nor forsake you." So we can confidently say, "The Lord is my helper; I will not fear; what can man do to me?" (Heb. 13:5–6, ESV)

WHAT OF THE SPIRIT

In this chapter, I would like to talk to you about a subject that had my husband and me contending for years. The topic is speaking in tongues. I saw things as a young person which made me uneasy; things which caused me to question the authenticity of the spiritual gifts. At one point in my youth, I went to a church where at the urging of the pastor, the entire congregation erupted in unknown tongues without interpretation. I felt very frightened and confused in that situation. I didn't understand what anyone was saying, and I certainly didn't see the point, except perhaps that each one was trying to act holier than the last, so the whole occurrence left a very bad taste in my mouth.

My brother told me about his experience in another church in Florida. He and his wife were told they must speak in tongues to prove that they were saved and filled with the Holy Spirit. They were actually given a sort of deadline in which they would have to either produce evidence of their salvation by speaking in tongues or leave the church. His wife succumbed to the pressure of that demand at the last moment and faked her way through, admitting to my brother later that she had been pretending, but he was too uncomfortable to do something he didn't feel led to do by God and ended up leaving the church before they could kick him out. He has not been one to go to church since. He still reads and studies his Bible, but has no church fellowship because he was so put off by that terrible experience.

I also have two sisters in Oregon who told me they had a similar experience where they went to a particular church for the first time, and while there, the congregation erupted in unknown tongues. They were frightened at first, and when no interpretation came following the exhibition, they felt left out of the loop as well. The whole experience was so disturbing that they never went back there again.

> If, therefore, the whole church comes together, and outsiders or unbelievers enter, will they not say that you are out of your minds? (1 Cor. 14:23, ESV).

I promise you that I never went back to the church that made me feel so uncomfortable, though on another occasion, I attended a tent revival with my, then, three-year-old son Aaron. At one point during the visit, he told me he had to go potty, so I took him around to the outside back of the tent where we witnessed certain people who had been "healed" of their ailments earlier in the evening meeting being paid off by one of the elders of the church. Naturally, later, when I heard others in the tent speaking in tongues and laying hands on some for healing, I assumed it was all a farce. For all I know now, those could have actually been instances of true healing, but after seeing what I had at the back of the tent, you couldn't have convinced me that I was witnessing the hand of God at work. I was jaded toward any so-called acts of the spirit for many years after due to those memorable experiences.

It is vital that the church does everything the way God intended, for His glory instead of for the almighty dollar; and for the edification of the church rather than to make one fellow look more spiritual than the other guy in the eyes of man, or else some folks who witness acts of ego or downright deception may be lost forever.

Thankfully, my husband did not give up on me and continued expounding to me about the gifts of the spirit and their purposes, or I would have lost an amazing opportunity to minister to others and to edify myself and the church. He explained that when one is given the gift of a specific tongue, the purpose is to bring someone to Christ, which is why we are to interpret and not to get caught up in the confusion that can come from misuse of a spiritual gift.

Our own personal prayer language is a different matter entirely and is between the person who is praying and God, but the gift of a tongue to persuade someone to Christ is a true miracle for the unbeliever, to bring him, or her to Christ; and not for the sake of the believer. Paul did not tell us not to pray in tongues, but warned us not to get swept away in misunderstanding. Tongues are a true gift of the Spirit when they are used correctly. Prophecy is also a gift of the Spirit, and Paul says that he desires especially that we would prophesy to build up the church.

> Pursue love, and earnestly desire the spiritual gifts, especially that you may prophesy. For one who speaks in a tongue speaks not to men but to God; for no one understands him, but he utters mysteries in the Spirit. On the other hand, the one who prophesies speaks to people for their up building and encouragement and consolation. The one who speaks in a tongue builds up himself, but the one who prophesies builds up the church. Now I want you all to speak in tongues, but even more to prophesy. The one who prophesies is greater than the one who speaks in tongues, unless someone interprets, so that the church may be built up.
>
> Now, brothers, if I come to you speaking in tongues, how will I benefit you unless I

bring you some revelation or knowledge or prophecy or teaching? If even lifeless instruments, such as the flute or the harp, do not give distinct notes, how will anyone know what is played? And if the bugle gives an indistinct sound, who will get ready for battle? So with yourselves, if with your tongue you utter speech that is not intelligible, how will anyone know what is said? For you will be speaking into the air. There are doubtless many different languages in the world, and none is without meaning, but if I do not know the meaning of the language, I will be a foreigner to the speaker and the speaker a foreigner to me. So with yourselves, since you are eager for manifestations of the Spirit, strive to excel in building up the church.

Therefore, one who speaks in a tongue should pray for power to interpret. For if I pray in a tongue, my spirit prays but my mind is unfruitful. What am I to do? I will pray with my spirit, but I will pray with my mind also; I will sing praise with my spirit, but I will sing with my mind also. Otherwise, if you give thanks with your spirit, how can anyone in the position of an outsider say

Amen to your thanksgiving when he does not know what you are saying? For you may be giving thanks well enough, but the other person is not being built up. I thank God that I speak in tongues more than all of you. Nevertheless, in church I would rather speak five words with my mind in order to instruct others, than ten thousand words in a tongue.

Brothers, do not be children in your thinking. Be infants in evil, but in your thinking be mature. In the Law it is written, By people of strange tongues and by the lips of foreigners will I speak to this people, and even then they will not listen to me, says the Lord. Thus tongues are a sign not for believers but for unbelievers, while prophesy is a sign not for unbelievers but for believers. If, therefore, the whole church comes together and all speak in tongues, and outsiders or unbelievers enter, will they not say that you are out of your minds? But if all prophesy, and an unbeliever or outsider enters, he is convicted by all, he is called to account by all, the secrets of his heart are disclosed, and so, falling on his face, he will worship God and declare that God is really among you. (1 Cor. 14:1–25, ESV)

When used incorrectly the gifts can cause confusion and Paul reminds us that God is not the author of confusion.

> For God is not a God of confusion but of peace, as in all the churches of the saints (1 Cor. 14:33, ESV).

Now that my unfounded fear of tongues has been assuaged, and I am comfortable using all spiritual gifts I see the benefit to all in the body of Christ for their use. Each of the gifts was designed to build up the church, to bring others to the knowledge of saving grace and to give God glory. Paul tells us that the gifts are a good thing and I for one want to be active in as many of those gifts as God is willing to bless me.

> Now concerning spiritual gifts, brothers, I do not want you to be uninformed. You know that when you were pagans you were led astray to mute idols, however you were

led. Therefore I want you to understand that no one speaking in the Spirit of God says "Jesus is accursed!" and no one can say "Jesus is Lord" except in the Holy Spirit.

Now there are varieties of gifts, but the same Spirit; and there are varieties of service, but the same Lord; and there are varieties of activities, but it is the same God who empowers them all in everyone. To each is given the manifestation of the Spirit for the common good. For to one is given through the Spirit the utterance of wisdom, and to another the utterance of knowledge according to the same Spirit, to another faith by the same Spirit, to another gifts of healing by the one Spirit, to another the working of miracles, to another prophesy, to another the ability to distinguish between spirits, to another various kinds of tongues, to another the interpretation of tongues. All these are empowered by one and the same Spirit, who apportions to each one individually as He wills. (1 Cor. 12:1–11, ESV)

As Christians, we should be working together as one to accomplish God's plan here on earth. To bring all who are lost into the kingdom. All the gifts of the Spirit are tools He has given us to achieve that end. We cannot be afraid to use the gifts He has given us, and we cannot be hesitant to go to Him as a body in prayer to stay forever in His will.

> Now you are the body of Christ and individually members of it. And God has appointed in the church first apostles, second prophets, third teachers, then miracles, then gifts of healing, helping, administration, and various kinds of tongues. Are all apostles? Are all prophets? Are all teachers? Do all work miracles? Do all possess gifts of healing? Do all speak with tongues? Do all interpret? But earnestly desire the higher gifts. And I will show you a more excellent way. (1 Cor. 12:27–31, ESV)
>
> And He gave the apostles, the prophets, the evangelists, the shepherds and teachers, to equip the saints for the work of the ministry, for building up the body of Christ, until we all attain to the unity of the faith and of the knowledge of the Son of God, to mature manhood, to the measure of the stature of the fullness of Christ, so that we

may no longer be children, tossed to and fro by the waves and carried about by every wind of doctrine, by human cunning, by craftiness in deceitful schemes. Rather, speaking the truth in love, we are to grow up in every way into Him who is the head, into Christ. (Eph. 4:11–15, ESV)

During the period of time when I was still uncomfortable with the idea of speaking in tongues, I was content to move in other gifts of the spirit and ignored the gift of tongues completely.

It was hard at that time to forget the examples I'd witnessed from those who were willing to pervert the gifts for their own gain. I'd finally gotten to a point where I had no problem with praying and thanking God for healing. I didn't balk at teaching or prophecy. I found that I had a constant "word of knowledge" flowing through my mind, which I knew was from the Lord, giving me access into the problems people were facing, and I had a prolific letter and note writing ministry to address those issues.

I received many phone calls from folks who had gotten a note from me, telling me they'd received a message at exactly the right moment and had been encouraged or helped in some way; though, I certainly cannot take credit for any of that, and I give God all the glory forever. In our years of ministry, and especially since the manifestation of healing I experienced after my first diagnosis, I have seen many miracles, but even after all these proofs and miracles, I was still loath to try speaking in tongues.

Then one day, I read something which changed my mind. A well-known pastor, T. D. Jakes, wrote that speaking in tongues when we are alone in our "prayer closet" is a unique gift. He continued by saying that though God is all knowing and can read our thoughts Satan cannot. Therefore, when we are having a problem and we discuss that problem out loud while praying to the Father, Satan hears about the issue as well and knows how to attack us in the coming days. When we pray in tongues only God understands what we are saying and that information is kept from the ears of Satan and his minions. This made more sense to me than anything

I'd ever heard on the issue of speaking in tongues, and it settled my mind on the issue.

I proceeded that night to experiment with the idea. I found when I was speaking in what to other people, I'm sure, would sound like gibberish, the things and people which were my major concerns played through my mind like a movie reel, and I could tell God was filtering back to me those things which were of importance to me that He had received in prayer. I knew God was hearing my prayers and I knew Satan didn't have a clue what was going on! I have included speaking in tongues in my personal prayer life ever since and it gives me a great deal of peace to be able to converse so freely with my Lord in our special language.

As a child of God I want every gift, every tool and every assurance God has promised us in His Word!

> And these signs will accompany those who believe: in my name they will cast out demons; they will speak in new tongues; they will pick up serpents with their hands; and if they drink any deadly poison. It will not hurt them; they will lay their hands on the sick, and they will recover. (Mark 16:17–18, ESV)

PRAYER, OUR GREATEST TOOL

Learning to pray is not nearly as difficult as it might seem. Reaching out to our Heavenly Father should be an easy conversation, though to someone new to the idea, it might feel a bit daunting. He isn't interested in fancy speeches or flowery soliloquies. He only cares about the issues of your heart, the gratitude you feel for the things He has done for you, and the subjects which are troubling you.

When we pray, we should be aware of our motives. Are we trying to force God's hand? Are we giving Him a sob story to make Him feel sorry for us? Are we threatening to stop following Him, or even loving Him if we don't get our own way? Do we pray believing our prayers are already heard, or do we feel we're just sort of throwing it out there to the universe and grasping at straws? Are we in constant prayer, or do we use prayer as a last resort?

Understand that if you do not pray, God will have nothing for which to respond. If you are asking for things which may harm you, or someone else, you are asking amiss. Sometimes God's answer to our prayers it "yes," sometimes it's "no" and sometimes it's "later." If we are indeed His beloved children, God does not want to answer our prayers with things that could hurt us, and He always sees the big picture, so He will protect us from ourselves and our misguided requests, whether we like it or not!

> What causes quarrels and what causes fights among you? Is it not this that your passions are at war within you? You desire and do not have, so you murder. You covet and cannot obtain, so you fight and quarrel. You do not have, because you do not ask. You ask and do not receive, because you ask wrongly, to spend it on your passions. (James 4:1–3, ESV)

Our Heavenly Father reads the motives of our hearts and can see the unbelief and doubt which lurks there. We must approach prayer with the faith to know we serve a God who has the power to answer our prayers, as long as the desire of our hearts is not just to fulfill our own lusts or hurt someone else. I said before that I used to think of God as some sort of big old Santa in the sky, and I asked for ridiculous things. I've met people who ask God for something outrageous and then decide that if He doesn't win the lottery for them or perform some other equally radical request, they will never look to Him again. He is our Father and just as your earthly parents, who love you and want what is in your best interest, would not give you everything you ask for because it wouldn't be good for you; our Heavenly Father God, who exists outside of time and can see everything in the total picture all at once, is even more diligent in guarding us from our own dark desires.

Grace is a commodity hard to define and something we do not deserve, but are given as a free gift due to His sacrifice and great love for us. When we approach God in prayer, we must believe that He is a God who wants to help us. Not only that He is able to help us, but that He truly wants to help us; that He has the power and the desire. When we truly understand that, then we can begin to grasp the concept that He rewards those who seek Him in faith believing.

> And without faith it is impossible to please Him, for whoever would draw near to God must believe that He exists and that He rewards those who seek Him (Heb. 11:6, ESV).

We must then have faith that the sacrifice He paid two thousand years ago covered our sins past, present, and future, and the price for our salvation, healing, mental soundness, and deliverance is already paid. Already covered means we don't have to beg for help. All we must do is pray in faith believing it is already finished, already done, already accomplished! Praise God He is faithful to fulfill His promises to us and is filled with love for His children.

> Let us hold fast the confession of our hope without wavering, for He who promised is faithful (Heb. 10:23, ESV).

RIGHTEOUS IN HIS EYES

"Many are the afflictions of the righteous, but the Lord delivers him out of them all" (Ps. 34:19, ESV).

This particular scripture used to throw me for a loop because I knew I wasn't the slightest bit righteous. Righteous means good, doesn't it? I couldn't be righteous, could I? Then I began to wonder. Who are the righteous?

I ran into an old friend recently. His father passed away a few months back and that loss devastated him. He was so very loved by his parents and had been especially close to his dad. Actually, I'd always been a bit jealous of their relationship, because my own childhood was less than fabulous. I thought he would lose his mind when his dad passed away, but he'd begun slowly to get back to normal. Then, recently, his wife was diagnosed with a terrible and terminal disease. She has been his best friend for many years, and unlike some of us, they didn't seem to need a period of adjustment in order to make things work in their marriage of decades. It always seemed they were made for each other, the best of friends and lovers, and now he is facing a future without his best girl.

We talked for some time, and my heart broke for this man, but when I reminded him God loves him, he told me he didn't believe that anymore. He knew God didn't care anymore, or else why was He making all of these terrible things happen to them? He reminded me he and his wife had taken in many foster children over the years and had always been the first couple to help whenever volunteers were needed at the church. He said after all the good things they'd done for Him (God), how could He let these things, life, happen to them? My friend told me they didn't deserve all the bad things they were getting, and he was very angry with God for all that they were being forced to endure.

You see, their lives had been so good for so many years that during those wonderful times, he thought they were being rewarded somehow for all the good they'd done, instead of just being blessed by a Father who loved them for being His children, just like I'd believed for so long I was being punished for all the bad I'd done in my past, instead of just reaping the earthly consequences of my own stupid mistakes. I tried to explain to him that God loves him, that He doesn't cause bad things to happen to us; that is Satan's job, and he works his evil through this fallen world, through disease and trouble with the help of his faithful minions. I tried to share with him that God is with him through this terrible time and that he needs to lean on His Father and on his brothers and sisters in Christ for strength and never stop having faith that God works on their behalf for good.

We talked about believing and not doubting and knowing that his wife's healing is already covered. They only need to receive and accept that gift, which was already provided over two thousand years ago.

I hope he was encouraged by the conversation, but what I took away from that exchange is that there are many people who still believe if they do good things, they will get good things, and if they do bad things, they will get bad things, which leaves them blindsided and confused when life happens. Where I'd always felt I wasn't good enough, clearly there are folks out there who feel like they are plenty good enough on their own.

On an earthly level, that "do bad, get bad" attitude makes sense and is entirely true as we do tend to be treated the way we treat others for the most part; but on a spiritual level, once we have trusted our Lord Jesus with our lives and eternity, we no longer get what we deserve, which is death; we get what Jesus deserves, which is life and more abundantly than we could have ever imagined!

I found it uncomfortable that my friend was so able to perceive of bad things happening to those who deserved bad since I'd considered myself one of those bad people for so long and he knew it, but that he'd decided he was a very good person in his own strength, who deserved nothing but good, thus, none of his current circumstances made sense to him. It is imperative that we as Christians share the good news of grace to a broken and troubled world. The hope which comes from the message of His love will save many lives. It is all about Him!

So, my answer to the question, "Who are the righteous?" is that the righteous aren't those who think they have done enough to earn their way into His good graces; the righteous are simply those who know the truth and have trusted Christ with their very lives.

> Therefore, as one trespass led to condemnation for all men, so one act of righteousness leads to justification and life for all men. For as by the one man's disobedience the many were made sinners, so by the one man's obedience the many will be made righteous. (Rom. 5:18–19, ESV)

Trying to explain to someone, who is going through hard times, that God is not "doing this to them" is difficult. We must remember no matter what, God is for us. He loves us. We might wonder what terrible things did I do to deserve this present situation, but understand, hardship comes because we live our earthly lives in a sinful world. Bad things happen to good people and to bad people, just like good things happen to good people and to bad people. The rain falls on the just and the unjust and the sun shines on the just and the unjust! When we belong to the Lord, He will use those terrible things, which the world lays on us, for our good, but we must trust Him and know that He is good *all* the time.

> But I say to you, Love your enemies and pray for those who persecute you, so that you may be sons of your Father who is in heaven. For He makes His sun rise on the evil and on the good; and He sends rain on the just and the unjust." (Matt. 5:44–45, ESV)
>
> Praise the Lord! Oh, give thanks to the Lord, for He is good! For His mercy endures forever. (Ps. 106:1, ESV)

Honestly, I was once in awe of this particular friend because he'd always seemed so sure of himself, but his surety was in his own ability, his own tough guy exterior, and the fact that his life had gone smoothly and been prosperous for so long before these recent troubles began. Now I can only have faith that God will reach him through His message of love, and he will come to the knowledge of that amazing grace available to him just for believing.

Marty and I had another friend who passed away about a year ago. Years before, she'd acted as one of the chaperones on a youth group trip we were heading up. We sat and talked one day while the youth were involved in an activity, and we asked her when she'd asked Jesus to be her Savior. She looked at us incredulously and said, "I've gone to church for as long as I can remember, and I've always been a good girl." She proceeded to expound on some of her good deeds, glorious attributes, and the kind things people always said about her. We tried gently to explain salvation through Christ and the whole conversation seemed to upset her.

Almost twenty years later, we met again at the cancer center. Very excited to see me, she grabbed me by the arm, and we sat and chatted until we had to go our separate ways to treatment. I made a point of calling her afterward and staying in touch. She told me that most of her friends had grown uncomfortable staying in contact with her when it looked as if the team at the cancer center were running out of feasible options. For months before she died, I called her daily to chat, and one day, she said she had a confession to make. She told me she'd felt superior somehow to Marty and I after the conversation we had twenty years ago when we'd both admitted to her how much we needed Jesus's love and forgiveness and that she had gone so far as to tell her elementary school-aged son not to associate with our son anymore because of it.

I was a bit surprised by her profession, though it did explain many things that had happened over the years, but I also had so much compassion for this woman that I didn't want to give up on her as so many had. I thought too that her confession might mean she was ready to hear more about saving grace through Christ Jesus's sacrifice.

I asked her if I could bring her some good books to read, and she told me not to bring them if they had anything to do with God. She was tired of people trying to "save her." She knew she was going to heaven because she had been such a good girl her whole life, and she'd always belonged to a church. She didn't want to talk about it anymore. I continued to call and visit clear up till the end, and I continued trying to share salvation through Jesus, but she wouldn't hear of it. My heart broke when she passed away, and I hoped someone was able to reach her before that dreadful end.

In my mind, there are three kinds of people in the world: those who have trusted and believed on Christ as Savior, those who think they are not good enough to ask for His grace, and those who don't think they need Him; whether they don't believe He exists, or they believe they've been good enough to deserve heaven on their own. The only ones who will be with Him when they leave this place are those who have trusted and believed on Him.

I've also heard of people who meet Jesus on their deathbed and have a conversion experience right before they die. I hope for her sake, Jesus came to her before she passed on. I will never stop mourning those who go to their death not knowing Christ, and I will never stop sharing the Jesus I have come to know and trust, with all my heart and soul, with everyone I meet along the way.

Many people have questioned me about what to do when you've prayed and your prayers don't seem to be getting answered. I would have to say first that we sometimes don't give God much time to answer prayers before we give up and turn somewhere else. Many prayers are thwarted by impatience.

Abram was seventy-five years old in Genesis 12:2 when God told him he would make of him a great nation. At that time, Abram and Sarai had no children. He was ninety-nine when God changed his name to Abraham and one hundred years old before Isaac was born to him. He waited twenty-five years for his prayer to be answered, but God answered his prayer!

Joseph was seventeen years old when his brothers sold him into slavery in Genesis 37:28. He was thirty years old before Pharaoh made him his second in command in Genesis 41:46. He waited thirteen years to receive the answer to his prayer, but God came through!

Daniel waited twenty-one days for an answer to prayer. God sent the answer to his prayer with an angel who was delayed by demonic forces. Michael the archangel came to the aid of the messenger in order to bring Daniel's reply. Twenty-one days, thirteen years, or twenty-five years might seem like a long time when we're waiting for an answer to come before we rise from our knees, but God is always good to His Word! One thing to keep in mind is that God is not slow in answering our prayers, but often the physical manifestation of that answer to prayer can be delayed due to opposing forces and circumstances that get in the way, sometimes by our own hand.

> Then he said to me, 'Fear not Daniel, for from the first day that you set your heart to understand and humbled yourself before your God, your words have been heard (Dan. 10:12, ESV).

He has promised that if we believe on Him, He is faithful to fulfill the promises He made to us. One of those promises is that He listens to our prayers.

> For the eyes of the Lord are on the righteous, and His ears are open to their prayer. But the face of the Lord is against those who do evil (1 Pet. 3:12, ESV).

Remember who the righteous are and don't be frightened by this scripture.

One of the most important things to remember when we go to God in prayer believing is not to change our minds! Stand fast. Don't alter your confession of faith! There is a danger in going back on your prayer. This is one of those places where faith is necessary; there can be no doubt!

> For now we live, if you are standing fast in the Lord. (1 Thess. 3:8, ESV)
>
> Since then we have a great High Priest who has passed through the heavens, Jesus, the Son of God, let us hold fast our confession. (Heb. 4:14, ESV)

And Jesus answered them, "Truly, I say to you, if you have faith and do not doubt, you will not only do what has been done to the fig tree, but even if you say to this mountain, 'Be taken up and thrown into the sea,' it will happen. And whatever you ask in prayer, you will receive, if you have faith." (Matt. 21:21–22, ESV)

Another of those promises is that we would have abundant life.

The thief comes only to steal and kill and destroy. I came that they may have life and have it abundantly (John 10:10, ESV).

But if we are expecting Him to give us an abundant life while we do earthly things that are not good for us, we are working at cross purposes. When we do things in the flesh, which are harmful for us, or against the law, we will pay earthly consequences for those actions. God does not promise to step in and save us from all of our self-inflicted, evil mess. We cannot expect to be covered with grace only so that we can do wicked things on purpose and be excused.

Don't think the grace you are given as a free gift is an excuse to do the wrong thing and then not pay consequences for those immoral acts.

> For you were called to freedom, brothers. Only do not use your freedom as an opportunity for the flesh, but through love serve one another (Gal. 5:13, ESV).

The Power of a Praying
Child of God

When a child of God prays, believing and not doubting, faith blossoms and grows. When Jesus departed this earth, He told us it was better for Him to go to be with the Father, because by departing, He would be able to send the Holy Spirit to be with us; a Spirit who would be in us, not just on us, or walking beside us, but in us, helping us and giving us power.

> And I will ask the Father, and He will give you another Helper, to be with you forever, even the Spirit of truth, whom the world cannot receive, because it neither sees him nor knows him. You know him, for he dwells

> with you and will be in you. (John 14:16–17,
> ESV)
>
> Nevertheless, I tell you the truth: it is to
> your advantage that I go away, for if I do not
> go away, the Helper will not come to you.
> But if I go, I will send Him to you. (John
> 16:7, ESV)

While He was here on this earth, Jesus walked among us, but when He left to join the Father, and the Father sent the Holy Spirit to help and comfort us, we were able to see the gift left to us through the sacrifice of Christ dying on the cross and rising again to conquer death. Now we can believe on the Son of God and the sacrifice He made for us to receive His Spirit, thereby becoming true children of God—heirs and joint heirs with Christ—filled with that very Holy Spirit! We receive that Spirit for a reason. We are to witness for Him to the ends of the earth!

> But you will receive power when the Holy
> Spirit has come upon you, and you will be my
> witnesses in Jerusalem and in all Judea and

Samaria, and to the end of the earth. (Acts 1:8, ESV)

The Spirit Himself bears witness with our spirit that we are children of God, and if children, then heirs—heirs of God and fellow heirs with Christ, provided we suffer with Him in order that we may also be glorified with Him. (Rom. 8:16–17, ESV)

Now that we have put our trust in Christ and are filled with the Holy Spirit, we have the power of our Lord coursing through us; the same power and more that He demonstrated when He walked on this earth. Imagine the things we can do together through Jesus for the Glory of God! It starts with prayer, a personal relationship with the God of the universe and the absolute knowledge that He is who He says He is and does what He says He does!

Once we understand the power of prayer, we then learn to pray, not just for ourselves, but for others. We don't pray because of an Old Testament law that tells us we must pray. We don't pray because we feel obligated to pray. We pray because our hearts are in tune with the heart of the Father, and He leads us in the desire to pray.

The longer I am in relationship with my Lord, the softer my heart becomes toward a hurting world. I find myself viewing things the way He views them, and my focus goes to prayer and support for those issues, which I know are close to His heart.

Marty and I pray together every day and then I pray throughout the day all day long. There are no rules for exactly how long you should pray, though I find that the more I pray, the more time I seem to have to get everything else done, even though admittedly it sounds as if the opposite should be true. The wording is completely your own. God doesn't care which words you use as long as you are communicating with Him.

It's even okay to tell God you're angry. I've done it lots of times and wasn't struck by lightning afterward. God's a big boy, and He can take your heartbreak and anger without getting His feelings hurt. In fact, He wants you always to be completely honest with Him! He will not, however, take orders from you on whom to strike down or destroy. I tried that one too, and it doesn't work. God would rather if you forgive as you've been forgiven.

So instead of praying for God to do bad things to people who have hurt you, try forgiving them and including them in your prayers each and every day. It is very difficult if not impossible to pray when your heart is filled with anger and bitterness; and it is virtually impossible to stay angry with someone you are praying for daily. Believe me, I've tried that one too.

> But I say to you, Love your enemies and pray for those who persecute you. (Matt. 5:44, ESV)
>
> Therefore I tell you, whatever you ask in prayer, believe that you have received it, and it will be yours. And whenever you stand praying, forgive, if you have anything against anyone, so that your Father also who is in heaven may forgive you your trespasses. (Mark 11:24–25, ESV)

When you pray, *believing* is the key! Confess with your mouth and believe with your heart. You remember:

> In nothing be anxious; but in everything by prayer and supplication with thanksgiving let your requests be made known unto God. And the peace of God, which surpasses all understanding, will guard your hearts and your minds in Christ Jesus. (Phil. 4:6–7, ESV)

Why must our prayer be made with thanksgiving? Thanksgiving means I know the prayer is already answered and the thing is already done! I am not worried about it any longer. I am not going to get the money, I already have it. I am not going to be healed, I am already healed. I have the money, my healing, my deliverance, because I have His Word, and His Word was already fulfilled two thousand years ago!

Your positive confession, your belief in His Word solves the problem. A wrong confession or a neutral confession is unbelief and hinders the Spirit's work in your body and in your life. Knowing that no word from God is void of power or fulfillment is important. Knowing that He watches over His Word to make it good is the confession of a victor. Your confession is your faith!

Your spirit always responds to your confession. Faith isn't a product of a logical mind, but of a recreated spirit. When you were born again, you received the very nature of the Father God. That nature grows and expands in you as you act on the Word. Your confession of the Father's perfect dominion in your body causes you to develop in ability and grace. As trials come into your life, your confession will either be in the realm of faith or in the realm of unbelief. Your confession either gives honor to God or to Satan.

Now you can see the importance of holding fast to, or standing fast in your confession. Your confession either makes you a conqueror, or it defeats you. We can only rise or fall to the level of our own confession. For your own sake, learn to hold fast to your confession even in the difficult times. Your confession either frees you or imprisons you.

> So if the Son sets you free, you will be free indeed (John 8:36, ESV).

The Son and His sacrifice have made you free, so stand fast in that freedom!

> For freedom Christ has set us free; stand firm therefore, and do not submit again to a yoke of slavery (Gal. 5:1, ESV).

STAND FAST THEREFORE

The time to make your confession is when you feel the attacks of Satan. When you feel the pain coming in your body, the anguish filling your mind, you see that your bank account is empty, but the bills are due, negative thoughts and insecurities whirl in your psyche. Reject the facts. Embrace the Truth! Command those thoughts to leave in the Name of Jesus. John Hagee has often said, "You can't keep the birds from flying over your head, but you can keep them from building a nest in your hair." Reject the negative thoughts. Your prayers are already answered; your needs are already met, just believe and receive grace from the Father.

> What then shall we say to these things? If God is for us who can be against us? (Rom. 8:31, ESV).

Your Heavenly Father is for you! Disease cannot conquer you; situations cannot master you; because we serve a God who is greater than any illness or circumstance. If you believe, His Spirit dwells in you!

> If the Spirit of Him who raised Jesus from the dead dwells in you, He who raised Christ Jesus from the dead will also give life to your mortal bodies through His Spirit who dwells in you (Rom. 8:11, ESV).

You have now learned what Paul preached; that in whatsoever situations or conditions you might find yourself, to rejoice in your victory continually!

> Not that I am speaking of being in need, for I have learned in whatever situation I am to be content. I know how to be brought low, and I know how to abound. In any and every circumstance, I have learned the secret of facing plenty and hunger, abundance and

need. I can do all things through Him who strengthens me. (Phil. 4:11–13, ESV)

By following the advice in this scripture, we are not celebrating the bad situations in our lives, but rather rejoicing through the turmoil, knowing that God is with us through it all. Paul knew that the only thing which truly mattered is unwavering faith, belief in an all powerful God who created the universe and loves His children. My God, your God, the God we know by the Name of Jesus. John knew that He who is in us is greater than all.

> Little children, you are from God and have overcome them, for He who is in you is greater than he who is in the world (1 John 4:4, ESV).

Please notice who you are! "You are of God." "You are born of God." "You are from God." You are a product of His will. He brought you forth through His Word. It is God who is at work within you, willing and working His own good pleasure.

> For it is God who works in you, both to will and to work for His good pleasure (Phil. 2:13, ESV).

Again, because we are in Him, once we have believed on Him and trusted Him, we have what He has. Is He sick? No He is not. Therefore when we believe, we are not sick. Is He poor? No He is not. Therefore when we believe, we are not poor. Is He worried? No, He is not worried. Therefore when we believe, we are not worried! Is He well and whole? Yes He is. Therefore when we believe, we are well and whole. Does He own the cattle on a thousand hills? Yes, He does. Therefore when we believe, we have all we need and more. We can have confidence in His love for us. If we are in Him and He is in us, then as He is so are we in this world. What a Savior!

> By this we know that we abide in Him and He in us, because He has given us of His Spirit. And we have seen and testify that the Father has sent His Son to be the Savior of the world. Whoever confesses that Jesus is the Son of God, God abides in him and he in God. So we have come to know and to

believe the love that God has for us. God is love, and whoever abides in love abides in God, and God abides in him. By this is love perfected with us, so that we may have confidence for the Day of Judgment, because as He is so are we in this world. There is no fear in love, but perfect love casts out fear. For fear has to do with punishment, and whoever fears has not been perfected in love. We love because He first loved us. If anyone says "I love God," and hates His brother, he is a liar; for he who does not love his brother whom he has seen cannot love God whom he has not seen. And this commandment we have from Him: whoever loves God must also love his brother. (1 John 4:13–21)

Recognize this fact: All is yours, or all is lost, by your confession. The secret of faith is the secret of confession. Faith says Jesus did it all and it is finished. Faith says that we have a thing before we see that we have it. Faith says we serve a God who called all into being by His spoken Word and He can heal all things, change all things, deliver all things, and fulfill all things by that same Word. Faith is foolishness to the world, but life to the believer. Faith says we believe the Truth, not the facts. Faith speaks before God acts. Declare health, favor, abundance, and deliverance; declare truth!

> And I pray that the sharing of your faith may become effective for the full knowledge of every good thing that is in us for the sake of Christ (Philem. 6, ESV).

God has taught me a wonderful faith secret. My faith will become effective (meaning things will happen through God), by my acknowledging of every good thing that is in me for the sake of Christ. All things are mine in Christ. Of His fullness I have received.

One of Satan's most subtle moves and therefore, one of his best tricks is to cause me to focus my attention upon myself, my past sins, my failures, and my weaknesses, all of my foolish mistakes, (of which there were many in my past). Now that I know more about his evil tricks, when I find myself dwelling on my past, I pause, rest in the Word, trust in the Lord, and resist the devil by saying, "In Jesus' Name." At the mention of Jesus's name, the devil must flee! Jesus is my very present help in times of trouble!

At revelation moments like these, my faith is virtually set on fire by acknowledging every good thing which is in me in Christ Jesus. What do I declare? I declare that I am who God says I am; that I have what God says I have and that I can do what God says I can do! Praise God! I have a report of victory, not a report of failure!

AFFIRMATION

An affirmation is a statement of fact. Faith and unbelief are each built up through affirmation. Affirmation of a doubt builds unbelief; the affirmation of faith works wonders to build strength and helps us believe even more. When we boldly affirm that the Word of God cannot be broken, we affirm that the Word and God are one. When we trust in the Word, we trust in God the Father also. When we believe the Word, we believe the Father also which leads to faith. Faith is shored up by belief, or short circuited by unbelief. Worry tears us down by increasing fear, and fear breeds unbelief. Believe therefore!

Abraham believed that God was able to perform all He promised. God did make good on His promise to Abraham. The amazing thing is that He took a man almost a hundred years old and renewed his body. He took a ninety-year-old woman and made her so young and beautiful that kings fell in love with her. She gave birth to her son after she was ninety years old. It wasn't Sarah's faith that made all this possible, it was Abraham's.

Doubt was a part of Sarah's life, as she made clear in her statement in Genesis 18:12:

> So Sarah laughed to herself, saying, "After I am worn out, and my lord is old, shall I have pleasure?"(ESV)

She was reprimanded by an angel and then she retreated in fear from the angel, as unbelief will always make us retreat.

Abraham's faith is what caused him to be righteous in the eyes of the Lord. He was not declared righteous by obeying law, after all the Mosaic Law did not exist in the time of Abraham and would not be written for 430 years. Abraham trusted and believed God and was afforded grace—the same grace available to us today just for believing in the promises made to us through the sacrifice of Jesus!

> What then shall we say was gained by Abraham, our forefather according to the flesh? For if Abraham was justified by works, he has something to boast about, but not before God. For what does the scripture say? Abraham believed God, and it was counted to him as righteousness. Now to the one who works, his wages are not counted as a gift but his due. And to the one who does not work but believes in Him who justifies the ungodly, his faith is counted as righteousness, just as David also speaks of the blessing of the one to whom God counts righteousness apart from works.
>
> Blessed are those whose lawless deeds are forgiven, and whose sins are covered; blessed is the man against whom the Lord will not count his sin.
>
> Is this blessing then only for the circumcised, or also for the uncircumcised? We say that faith was counted to Abraham as righteousness. How then was it counted to him? Was it before or after he had been circumcised? It was not after, but before he

was circumcised. He received the sign of circumcision as a seal of the righteousness that he had by faith while he was still uncircumcised. The purpose was to make him the father of all who believe without being circumcised, so that righteousness would be counted to them as well, and to make him the father of the circumcised who are not merely circumcised but who also walk in the footsteps of the faith that our father Abraham had before he was circumcised.

For the promise to Abraham and his offspring that he would be heir of the world did not come through the law but through the righteousness of faith. For if it is the adherents of the law who are to be the heirs, faith is null and the promise is void. For the law brings wrath, but where there is no law there is no transgression. (Rom. 4:1–15, ESV)

Notice that the scripture says, "For the law brings wrath, but where there is no law there is no transgression." If there is no law governing a thing, then we are not transgressing a law by not adhering to it. In Germany on their highway system which is called the autobahn, there are no posted speed limits. I lived there for approximately five years, many years ago. When I initially arrived, I found it unnerving to drive so fast, but quickly got used to that freedom. Due to the fact that there were no posted speed limits, I didn't get stopped no matter how fast I was flying! Once I arrived back in the United States where the roads have posted speed limits, I was stopped quite frequently for breaking the speed limit, (and occasionally for breaking the sound barrier). I received several tickets and had to readjust my thinking. Faith depends on grace. It is not determined by what I do, but by what I believe, again I had to readjust my thinking.

> That is why it depends on faith, in order that the promise may rest on grace and be guaranteed to all his offspring-not only to the adherent of the law but also to the one who shares the faith of Abraham, who is the father of us all, as it is written, "I have made you the father of many nations"—in the presence of the God in whom he believed, who gives life to the dead and calls into existence the things that do not exist. (Rom. 4:16–17, ESV)

In Matthew 17 and Mark 9, we read an account of a father coming to Jesus for help. His son is mute and has seizures so bad that he falls into the fire and into the water all the while foaming at the mouth. The father recognizes that the problem is caused by an evil spirit, so he comes to the disciples for help. The disciples are not able to cast out the demon, and Jesus chastises them for their lack of belief, then He says that all things are possible if we believe. Not some things, but all things!

> And Jesus said to him, "If you can! All things are possible for one who believes." Immediately the father of the child cried out and said, "I believe; help my unbelief!" (Mark 9:23–24, ESV)

After Jesus casts out the evil spirit, he helps the child up and sends him on his way, with his father, healed and whole. Then the disciples come to Him.

> And when He had entered the house, His disciples asked Him privately, "Why could we not cast it out?" And He said to them, "This kind cannot be driven out by anything but prayer." (Mark 9:28–29, ESV)

Faith is like a muscle and must be exercised. We exercise that muscle by believing and praying. Are you exercising your faith, or are you dominated by unbelief? Don't allow unbelief to be victorious in your life.

As Christians, we should constantly affirm that Jesus is to us the guarantee of the New Testament and that every Word from the Bible can be faithfully depended on as truth. Then, when that Word is on your lips, it is as if God is speaking. Now don't get me wrong. I am not claiming to be God. I am simply saying that His Word on our lips carries power; it never grows old, is never weak, never loses its authority, and is always the true living Word—the life-giving Word. So, when you boldly confess it, it becomes a living thing in your mouth, and you are able to do mighty things in the name of the God who sent you.

A wonderful fact is that your word can indeed become one with God's Word. His Word living in you gives you authority in heaven. The words on your lips are the words that live in you and dominate you.

This "seen" Word gives faith in the unseen Word sitting at the right hand of the Father. The Word carries you beyond sense knowledge, and into the very presence of God, and gives you the right to stand before Him.

We, as human beings, are always confessing something, affirming something; sometimes, those affirmations can be disastrous to our lives. When we affirm things such as, "I just can't do it," "I don't feel like I'll ever get over this illness," "This will be the thing that kills me," or, "We're broke, and I don't see how we're going to come up with the money," you are expressing your doubt in God's ability and desire to take care of you. You are for all intents and purposes expressing your faith in unbelief.

People who constantly confess their faith in disease, failure, and tragedy will have lives filled with disease, failure, and trouble. Our words have power—the power to direct our lives, to build us up or tear us down. Instead affirm these things: "The Lord is my shepherd, I do not want;" "My Father is greater than all;" "God is the strength of my life, of whom shall I be afraid?" "If God be for you, who can be against you?" and one of my all time favorites, "By His stripes, I am healed." Jesus said, "Heaven and earth may pass away, but My Word will never pass away." Know that His Words have the power to save, to heal and to make good all of His promises forever.

I often heard a phrase in church that went something like, "God said it. I believe it. That settles it." My husband and I heard many pastors in our circle of influence use that statement, and it always bothered me. One day, when my husband and I were talking he said, "The reason it bothers you is because it isn't true. It should be God said it. That settles it. It doesn't matter if we believe it or not. If God has said it, it is true!" I have a very wise husband.

WONDER WORKING WORDS

As I've said before, our words are powerful living things. Whether in prayer, or in your everyday life, the things we say invite success or attract disappointment. Use your words to change your life! Declare health, favor, and abundance. Have a continual report of victory on your lips. Be the positive encourager God designed you to be. You are surrounded by those who desperately need that encouragement.

I write notes and send texts to those I love and care about, every day and on the rare occasion that something comes up which prevents me from doing that I get concerned phone calls and texts from many who wonder if I'm all right. I've discovered that many family and friends have come to depend on that bit of daily encouragement from me. What a small and seemingly insignificant gesture and yet what a blessing to so many, why would I stop doing something which has so many positive consequences when I have the power to make so many happy with so tiny a gift?

What can you do to lift someone up today? You have the power to make a real difference in someone's life with a word, a smile, a hug, a note or some other simple act.

If you have a wayward child, speak life, love, and success over your child's life; be a ray of favorable confirmation in that child's day; believe me, there will be negative forces aplenty. If you are dissatisfied with your job, living arrangements, financial circumstances, a spouse, or your own health, habits, and practices, you will make a far bigger and better difference by speaking positive words of affirmation into the situation. Remember that Satan is listening too. He will use every pessimistic word out of your mouth to attempt destruction in your life and the lives of the people you care about. Don't give Him fuel for his evil fires by speaking failure into your life or the lives of your family members.

When my husband and I were ministering to a church in a close by community some time ago, we did quite a bit of counseling for families and couples as one of our pastoral duties. We always told people if they came to us we would give them only biblical advice for the problems they presented, so they shouldn't expect anything else.

A man and his teenage daughter began to come in for regular sessions, and after we talked for awhile, we asked them to do some assignments together during the coming week and to read together certain passages from the Bible in the days between sessions. Every week, they returned for their next meeting, and we asked if they had done their assignments or read the Bible together as we'd invited them to do, and the dad would tell us he didn't have time, that he couldn't fit it into his schedule, that the problem was simply that his daughter was a bad seed and just like her mother, that she would never change, that she would continue getting into trouble no matter what he did.

He predicted she would get pregnant or end up in prison and ruin his life. We asked him if he'd ever tried speaking positive things into his daughter's life, and he told us all she ever brought him was trouble, and he couldn't come up with anything positive to say about her.

We continued giving the same advice, trying to encourage the girl and attempting to help her understand how much God loved her.

He ignored all we said and finally quit coming to see us. We subsequently advised that perhaps they needed more help than we could give if they weren't willing to hear the truth of God's Word, but the father never got his daughter the help she needed and continued to speak failure and defeat into her life day after day and year after year.

A couple of years later, his daughter did become pregnant. He tried to compel her to abort the baby, but she refused. Finally, he told her he wouldn't help her or allow her to stay in his house if she didn't listen, and he forced her to give up the infant. The young lady languished for some time, turning to drugs and men and then finally took her own life. This case was a perfect example of the damage which can be done by negative affirmation over and over in a young person's life. I can't help but wonder how much difference a few kind and understanding words might have made in the life of that girl; if her father confessing God's love over her life would have given her the hope to go on?

As I said before, Satan is listening. If our words are filled with negative affirmation, he has more destructive ammunition to use against us. Our words, or our testimony, must be in harmony with God's Word, or we are giving an advantage to the enemy. The Bible says we overcome the devil by the Word in our testimony.

> And they have conquered him by the blood of the Lamb and by the Word of their testimony for they loved not their lives even unto death (Rev. 12:11, ESV).

Our words can work wonders, or inflict pain. Words in harmony with the Word of God can work wonders. Words that are not in line with the Word of God will cause chaos in our lives and the lives of others.

> Let no corrupting talk come out of your mouths, but only such as is good for building up, as fits the occasion, that it may give grace to those who hear (Eph. 4:29, ESV).

My words in line with God's Word can lift up and give hope, but if my words are the words of the world they can destroy and dash all hopes.

Words have creative power. God, through Jesus, spoke the very universe into being. He created all things, which were created, by His spoken Word. Don't ever doubt the effect of your words on your faith confession, or the power you have to influence someone else's life.

I challenge you to never give in to the adversary. Watch over your words. Remember that you serve a God who is the master of your situations. Jesus met defeat and conquered it. You will face defeat everywhere that you go, but you too can face that defeat as a master in Jesus' Name and overcome. In the Name of Jesus you conquer Satan! Don't give up. Don't give in. God is for you and you can't be conquered as long as you believe in His promises!

HAVE YOUR OWN FAITH

I used to depend on another's faith in times of need. All those years ago as a child, when I didn't believe God was listening to my prayers, I depended on the prayers of Pastor Brown and his wife. Once he was gone from my life, I knew I wasn't good enough to deserve God's attention, so I floundered, lost, for many years. After I married my husband Marty, I leaned on him and on his prayers. I knew he was a good man and figured God must certainly be listening to him when he prays. I guess you could call me a faith hitchhiker. I was always waiting for someone to pray the "prayer of faith" for me since I knew my own prayers would most definitely fall on deaf ears.

DONNA M. YOUNG

I no longer believe that God doesn't hear my prayers. Now I speak with my Father every day. Now I am filled with the faith of God. Now when a crisis comes I do my own praying. If sickness strikes I am ready to be used by God to minister healing in Jesus' Name. God has given me the measure of faith.

> For by the grace given to me I say to everyone among you not to think of himself more highly than he ought to think, but to think with sober judgment, each according to the measure of faith that God has assigned. (Rom. 12:3, ESV)

I have the measure of faith, so do you! Each of us, if we are a believer, has the measure of faith. As Christians, we have the right to go boldly before the throne of God in prayer, in Jesus' Name. But, we must ask, seek, and knock. Though it is wonderful to have the prayers of others, no one can effectively do your praying for you.

> Ask, and it will be given to you, seek and you will find, knock and it will be opened to you. For everyone who asks receives, and the one

who seeks finds, and to the one who knocks it will be opened. (Matt. 7:7–8, ESV)

As a child of God, you have the right to approach Him. You have as much right as any of His children to pray and be heard. You are His beloved and His favored one. Though you are His favored one, God doesn't have a teacher's pet, so your prayers are every bit as important as the prayers of any evangelist, missionary, teacher, or even your pastor.

So Peter opened his mouth and said: "Truly I understand that God shows no partiality, but in every nation anyone who fears Him and does what is right is acceptable to Him." (Acts 10:34–35, ESV)

Because I have developed my own prayer life, I no longer feel the need to ask someone else to do my praying. Other's prayers are lovely, but I know that I have instant access to the Father, and so do you! While prayer used to be my last resort, it is now my first instinct. Now I pray continually, not that I am in competition with anyone about who might pray the longest, but I wake in the morning and speak with my Father and continue to carry on a conversation with Him throughout the day. Now there isn't a single part of my day or life that I don't want to share with Him.

A prayer can be as short as, "Help me Lord," and sometimes those are the most effective prayers, or as long as you wish. For me, the continual prayer works best because I know He is my best friend; I know I mess up often enough to need His help in an ongoing fashion, and I love being in contact with Him all throughout the day. I also find it supportive to remember He is always with me, because it helps me to behave myself and, at all times, try to represent my Lord in a good light to anyone I meet.

Since I was born into less than desirable circumstances, sometimes my responses can tend to be a bit crass if I am not diligent to censor them. When we're mistreated as children, we can tend to carry odd traits into our adult lives. Feeling the need as a young person to cover up my insecurities with a brazen attitude—one which would make me appear more in charge—I have tended to be a bit opinionated and loud as an adult, so that is an issue

I continue to deal with. A therapist once told me that having no control over our circumstances when we are small can lead to controlling behaviors when we're grown, so I try every day, with God's infinite wisdom and help, to keep an eye on my desire to control everything around me. He is also working on my patience, to help on the days where that isn't working very well.

> Rejoice in hope, be patient in tribulation, be constant in prayer (Rom. 12:12, ESV).

I also believe now that my prayers are answered. I know that Jesus' sacrifice two thousand years ago was a promise for us, for me. I don't believe that my prayers will be answered someday. I believe they are already answered.

> In that day you will ask nothing of me. Truly, truly, I say to you, whatever you ask of the Father in My Name, He will give it to you (John 16:23, ESV).

Each day I proclaim: I will use the power given to me in the name of my Lord Jesus to pray mighty prayers. I will be the courageous channel of God's blessing to minister hope and healing to whoever He places in my path. I have the faith of God. I am the righteousness of God in Christ. God loves me!

I feel like I can't say this enough. Don't forget the devil hears you too. The words you speak on a daily basis, or when you pray (unless you are praying in tongues) are just as audible to Satan as they are to God. If your prayers are filled with begging, doubt and whining, they are the perfect vehicle for Satan to use in attacking you. If your prayers are positive, grateful prayers, you leave him little useable ammunition.

When we pray about sickness, instead of praying: "Oh God, I am so sick, and I just don't know how I'm going to get any better. Please help me, God. I've tried to be good, and I think I deserve some good news here." Try praying, "Father God, the report from the doctor wasn't very good today, but that's okay, because I know that by the stripes Jesus bore I am healed. Thank you, Father, for your promises and thank you that you watch over your promises to see them fulfilled. I praise you God for loving me and for providing everything I will ever need. Amen."

Satan has a much harder time attacking us when we don't hand him the ammunition with which to do it.

You will be much more filled with joy if you spend your time thanking God for what you do have instead of complaining about what you don't have. An attitude of gratitude is a wonderful thing and makes you a much more pleasant person to be around.

I said earlier that I didn't know how my husband managed to stay with me during the first years of our marriage. I know I was a difficult person to be around. My sisters have told me what a "bossy pants" I was when we were kids, while I was running a household and taking care of my siblings, as our mother steadily succumbed to the hell which is alcoholism.

I carried that bossy pants nature with me into adulthood. I felt more comfortable being in control of my circumstances, and I ended up in a number of management positions with businesses and large corporations as I utilized my natural ability to "rule and reign" in whatever situation I found myself. I was miserable all the time. I had a bleeding ulcer and a nervous nature born out of that need to be in control, but God, (Oh how I love those "but God" moments), is changing me.

He has managed little by little to turn me from an angry, nagging, controlling wife, mother, and sibling to a gentler person little by little. Now, I won't go so far as to say there isn't still work to be done, but gratefully He isn't done with me yet. I thank Him and praise Him for restored relationships with family members who felt as though I had bullied them into submission in former years, and I look forward to the years we still have together.

I have realized through God's love that I was putting myself in positions of power to quell the feelings of helplessness that engulfed me as a small abused child. He had to teach me how to allow Him to fight my battles and how to stop trying to be in charge of everyone around me. Sometimes the biggest battles we fight are the ones taking place in our own minds; those spiritual battles can be the most devastating. When we think we know more than God, we put ourselves in a very precarious position.

> For the weapons of our warfare are not of the flesh but have divine power to destroy strongholds. We destroy arguments and every lofty opinion raised against the knowledge of God, and take every thought captive to obey Christ, being ready to punish every disobedience, when your obedience is complete. (2 Cor. 10:4–6, ESV)

These days, I find that I want to be an encourager. If you spend any time at all around me, I will likely remind you of how much God loves you. I will share the Gospel with anyone willing to listen, and if you tell me you aren't worthy, or that you've made too many mistakes, I will explain to you that God's grace is stronger than any mistakes you've ever made; and that as long as you believe, you are indeed His beloved and His favored one. All you have to do is look at someone like me, who has messed up as much as any one person can and who knows now, that because God is love, He loves me! What a blessing to know you are loved by your creator!

MAKE YOURSELF AVAILABLE

Look around you! There is always someone worse off, more lonely or hurt, than you are; someone who needs encouragement or prayer. During my hours upon hours at the cancer center in the past five plus years, I have met hundreds of people who are at the end of their proverbial rope. I've made, and lost to disease, countless new friends.

I am honored to say I've helped to lead many to the Lord before they lost their battle. Though it's hard to see anyone lost to cancer, knowing that they came to know Jesus before they left this place makes the parting less painful. We will meet again. And for each new believer brought into the kingdom, I like to imagine Satan with a big fat black eye!

God created us to be social beings. We need one another in order to feel whole. Put yourself out there with the message of the grace of God, the true Gospel, and change lives.

Remember, it isn't our job to judge the person God puts in our path. It isn't our job to decide whether we believe them to be worthy of our prayers or God's help. It is only our job to pray. I used to selfishly pray for miracles for myself, wealth, fame, and material things since I had come from very little; until I began to notice all the miracles already existing in my life and in the lives of those around me. Once I became more grateful for those things I already had, I realized I didn't truly want many of the things I'd been praying for all those years. Now that I'm aware God hears my prayers and that He provided all I need two thousand years ago, it has been easier to stop concentrating on me.

Now I want to be the miracle in someone else's life; the tool God uses to reach another believer for His glory, the hand He uses to heal. God's hand is on me, and through that revelation, I can extend that hand of God to others. There is nothing in this world quite as wonderful as being used by God.

I met one woman about a year and a half ago who was being ravaged by liver cancer. We talked and I discovered she was not a believer, but she needed a friend. I tried talking to her about the Lord a couple of times, but she made it abundantly clear she didn't want to hear anything about God. I didn't push, but I also knew, through asking around, she didn't have a husband or children and was very much alone in the world, so I made myself available and between her hospital stays, we began to hang out and spent lots of time together having lunch and visiting local sights. She especially loved garage and rummage sales.

She could be a little difficult sometimes, as we all are, but I knew she was in a great deal of pain, so I tried to be patient in return. I helped her move her bedroom at home down onto the main floor so she would be closer to the restroom since her chemo was causing lots of problems in that area. After that move, when she was in the hospital again, I visited her and brought her small gifts along with lots of hugs and smiles. On one such visit, I gave her a

Bible and some booklets introducing her to the idea of a grace message.

Our relationship went on in this way for about six months, and she became increasingly dependent on me for companionship and rides, which was perfectly fine with me. She talked to me about her childhood in a home that didn't worship God. She explained that her parents hadn't been believers, and when a school friend had invited her to attend church, her parents refused to let her go, so she'd grown up with a strong prejudice against people who seemed religious. I explained to her that there is a difference between religion and a relationship with Jesus and told her we aren't crazy about religious people either, which seemed to put her more at ease.

She had one brother who was dealing with his own very serious health problems, receiving kidney dialysis twice a week and lived quite far away; and two nieces who never visited her even though they would be the beneficiaries of her will, so when we weren't together, we were talking on the phone and making plans for our next outing. I became her only lifeline. As her condition grew worse and her hospital stays became more frequent and lengthy, she grew more frightened about what the future might hold. Finally, in His perfect timing, she began to ask me questions about God, heaven, and death.

One day, when I came for a regular visit, she placed her hand on mine and asked me how she could be sure she would be in heaven with Jesus when she died. I led her in the sinner's prayer. We cried together and held each other. I told her how much I loved her and how much God loved her. The next day, she passed away. Knowing my friend was reconciled with God and not relegated to an eternity in hell is worth every moment of what many might consider months of inconvenience. I know I will see her again when I leave this place.

Some might say, "Why would you keep trying to share Jesus with her when she obviously didn't want to hear? That just seems hard, and I wouldn't want to be pushy." I'm here to say that we will go through many "hard" things in our lives, situations, and experiences that will take us up and down, but as Joyce Meyer, a noted evangelist, would say, "God has anointed us for hard!"

I will say again that if I truly believe Jesus is the best thing that has ever happened to me, and I do, then how I could not want to share Him with others is beyond me. And if I truly believe that the only way any of us will get to heaven is through Him, and I do, then how could I not help others to know Him better? How could I consider myself a believer, a follower of Christ, and not have the growth of the kingdom of God as my greater purpose?

Another account I remember has to do with a man who was a member of a church my husband and I served as pastors for a number of years. We had recently been called to this particular congregation, and Marty and I always made a practice of visiting the home bound, prisoners, nursing home residents, and those in the hospital throughout the community wherever we lived and served. This man's wife passed away immediately after we came to the church and her funeral was my husband's first official act in the new pulpit.

The sweet old fellow had spent so many years caring for his ailing wife that once she was gone, he felt he had no purpose left and his own health decreased rapidly. We visited him often and took him meals, but each time we went to see him, he seemed to slip further away. We got a call one Friday night and found out he'd been admitted to the hospital. We found him in critical care wearing an oxygen mask over his face and a panicked look in his eyes. We began gently to try to discern what was causing him such obvious dread.

Eventually, we discovered that even though he'd been a member of that particular church for over fifty five years since he'd married his wife, he had no idea where he would go when he left this place. Shocked that no one in his life, especially his church life, had ever explained grace to this man, or introduced him to Jesus, we spoke to him of spiritual things. Telling him about Jesus, we gladly introduced him to his redeemer. He asked what it would be like to die, and Marty told him it would be the same as walking through a door, right into the arms of Jesus. By the time we left that day, the look of panic had left his eyes.

The following Sunday, right after services were over at the church, we got a call from his family telling us he had just passed away. We were honored to have been able to share Jesus with him and grateful we'd been able to reach him before he died. Marty shared the story of his questions and redemption at his funeral, and after the service was finished, we had two people come up to us and ask if they could talk to us about salvation. God is so good and He truly does use every tragedy in our lives for good in some way if we love Him and are the called according to His purpose!

While it is honorable that the man loved and cared for his wife, it is also sad that taking care of his wife's health was his only purpose. We all know that a life without purpose has no meaning and feels cold and empty. A life centered in Christ is filled with meaning and contains His ultimate purpose, that all should know Jesus. I can't help but think that if this man's life had been filled with the joy of sharing Christ, he would not have been so devoid of hope after losing his wife. We must share with the world that there is more to being a Christian than the mere act of calling ourselves one.

Many people have come to the false assumption that if they sit in a church pew, or try to be a good person, they will be in heaven when they leave this place. I don't want to be a buzz kill, but nothing could be farther from the truth. Sitting in a church won't make you a Christian any more than sitting in a garage will make you a car, or sitting in McDonald's will make you a cheeseburger. Jesus is the way, the truth, and the life. No one comes to the Father but through Him! No other religion, no other gods, no other practices will do. We can't be good enough to earn our way to salvation, and once we trust Him for salvation, we can't do anything bad enough that will cause us to lose our salvation. He loves us. He already did it *all*.

Once you belong to Him, you are His forever and entitled to every promise He has provided for His children! Some have told us that when we preach this way of grace we are sharing cheap grace, but I couldn't disagree more! Nothing about the way Jesus suffered and died was insignificant or cheap. His death and resurrection was the most noteworthy event in all of history. We only cheapen it by suggesting that there is any act that we as human beings could perform which would add to its value. He is the only way!

> Jesus said to him, "I am The Way, and The Truth, and The Life. No one comes to the Father except through Me." (John 14:6, ESV)

As For Me and My House

In our own lives, Marty and I made plenty of mistakes. All those years of inflicting the mixed message of grace and law on our own children had its repercussions. Our kids had a tough time trying to measure up to the unrealistic expectations we had for them.

My daughter Liz once told me, "I'm so tired of you trying to live vicariously through me. Get your own life!" And rightly so! I'd been laying ridiculous hopes on her for many years. This is the same young woman, who at the age of four was sitting in a church pew, and when she was wiggling around, I said to her, "Elizabeth, we're in church. Is that the way Jesus would want you to act?" And she responded with, "I don't care! I hate Jesus!" loud enough for the entire congregation to hear. On another occasion, when Dad and I were in the kitchen talking, she walked in and upon hearing our conversation burst out with, "Jesus, Jesus, Jesus, is that all you two ever talk about?"

Once I began to let go and trust God to work in her life, she fared much, much better and has grown to be a lovely, strong, talented, godly woman and friend. I gladly share that she is in a place spiritually that I didn't even know existed at her age and gives great Christian advice to any who come seeking.

Our son Dave pulled away so hard we thought we'd lost him at one point. We even talked briefly about sending him to a military school since I didn't know how much longer I could handle his verbal abuse and constant troublemaking, and that made me very sad as he'd been such a loving, great kid most of his life.

We changed our minds when we decided that, as his parents, we couldn't just give up on him and needed to see things through. As the pastor's kid, he'd wanted to be popular and wanted his peers to like him. We'd pushed so hard from the other direction, with all of our legalistic expectations; he started to get in the types of trouble, which would follow him for several years.

David eventually joined the Marines, ironically, and after basic training and MOS schooling, served in Afghanistan. He still serves, though in the States now. He is buying his own home, works with Dad doing construction and painting, and has become a strong, dependable, loving, and honorable young man who worships with us every week when he is not gone for military service.

Aaron, my oldest son, was in and out of trouble for decades, even including some time in prison. I feared for his life on more than one occasion. He has been divorced several times and lost touch with most of his children. I felt tremendous guilt for modeling behaviors, through failed marriages, which I realized later might have led him to believe marriage is a disposable entity. Regardless of how I was treated in those situations, I felt I should have tried harder and put up with more to be a better role model. I realize now that me staying in situations where I was abused, mistreated, and cheated on would have sent the wrong message.

His last marriage ended tragically in divorce, but this time, he remained active in his children's lives. He is a good dad and all three of the children from that union have trusted Jesus as their Savior. He is a hard worker and loves his family. God is good! I know that the message of grace has been a source of peace and joy in the more recent lives of our children and grandchildren, and I am grateful for that blessing.

Marty's son Jarrod lived with us for some time and had difficulties with school and in making friends, but we helped him with homework, encouraged him, and got him involved in some extracurricular activities at school. Jarrod went on to complete high school and some college courses. He has grown to be a godly man, married to a godly woman named Stephanie and has two beautiful children who love Jesus. I could go on to tell you about some of the challenges they have faced, but I will save that for another time. Suffice it to say that they have come to trust the Lord for everything in their lives.

I can't begin to tell you how very thankful I am for the hand of God in the lives of our kids. Where once I saw disaster, now I see God's Word coming to fruition, if only slowly in some cases. I know He is much wiser than I, and He loves our kids in ways I can't even imagine. I still try to stay connected with their lives, and sometimes, it can be construed as butting in, I suppose, but I am learning to let go and let God.

In our years of providing family counseling in various churches, we were told by many parents, "You two always seem to have the perfect answers. Thank you. Your kids are lucky to have you as parents." At this point in the conversation, we would usually look at each other and break out in uncontrolled laughter. We have explained on numerous occasions that our own kids were our unsuspecting lab rats for many years. We'd already made every conceivable error in the realm of raising young ones, which was possible to commit, and that they, as congregants, were benefiting from the mistakes we'd made with our own children. The advice we give these days is directly from the Bible, combined with our own, sometimes costly, personal experiences, and now when applied with a loving hand of grace is the best parenting guidance we could ever hope to provide.

Our own kids would tell you that they knew their parents were the strictest parents in town, but though they snuck out on occasion to do what they wished and paid the consequences later; they were also grateful their friends knew us and that they had an acceptable "out" to keep them from some of the more outrageous activities offered to them. Often they stayed out of trouble by simply telling their friends we would kill them if they got caught, and truthfully, back in those days, we probably would have! We often used their mistakes and troubles, along with our own, as material for sermons, much to their chagrin.

Frankly, if I could do it all over again, I would have treated my children with the same grace and love my Lord has afforded me, and I'm sure their lives would've been more stress free. I can't go back and change things for us, but I can share with you that your children probably already feel the weight of the world on their shoulders and are more critical of themselves than you might remember being when you were young.

There's plenty of stress, guilt, and self-loathing going on in the world, especially the world our youth inhabits. Be their loudest cheerleaders. Be their advocates. Teach them the Word. Share the grace of God with them. Remind them that Jesus loves them and that they are the righteousness of God in Christ. Fill their minds and hearts with reasons to celebrate the rest and peace of Christ, and you will have young people who are ready to face the world and handle all it throws at them.

Most of all, teach them through example how to experience joy through all things by keeping their eyes on Jesus, and they will learn how to truly rejoice and praise God. That alone will give them strength that they can never find in the world.

A Few Things

In my years on this earth and through the many varied situations I've experienced, I've learned a few things I'd like to share:

- Our lives are filled with choices. We can choose whether or not we want Jesus in our lives and whether or not to trust Him for salvation. To me, this one is an easy choice, but it is still a choice.

- Forgiveness is a choice. We can choose to live in misery being angry all the time, or be freed by letting go of the anger that has engulfed us. I choose forgiveness, thereby setting myself free.

- Joy is a choice. When we wake up in the morning, we can choose to be in a good mood or a bad one. The face I show the world will have an effect on those I encounter and could help them to make a decision for Christ. My mood will also drastically affect the way my day will evolve. I choose joy.

- Kindness is a choice. How I treat people reflects on me, but also reflects on the God I serve. I choose to treat people the way I want to be treated. I choose kindness.

- Love is a choice. I serve a God who is Love, but I can choose to emulate Him or not. Love is what attracted me to my Lord in the first place, and it is what has made me adore Him and want to share Him with everyone I meet. I choose love, because I choose Christ.

- Giving is a choice. We can usually tell what is important to someone by what they give their money and time to. I want to give to those things that are on the heart of my Father. I choose giving because it impacts lives and because it feels so good!

- It is ridiculous to argue with people about what they like. Everyone is entitled to their own opinion, and not everyone's opinion has to be the same as mine (this was a difficult one for me). I actually used to have conversations that went something like this:

> Me: I don't like cooked spinach.
>
> You: I love cooked spinach with a little salt and lemon.

Me: How can you like cooked spinach?
That sounds disgusting!

Yes, I was trying to tell someone they were not allowed to like something, because I didn't like it! You can't *make* people agree with you. I also cannot make you love Jesus and trust Him for salvation; again, that is your choice.

- We come and go so quickly. I've lost so many loved ones to death: My mom, my stepdad, my father, a sister, a son, a brother-in-law, grandparents, aunts and uncles, and so many friends and church members. Some of them knew Jesus and some of them didn't. My heart breaks when I imagine that there are some who are not in heaven and that I might have been able to share Jesus with them if I'd known the wonderful love and grace of Christ sooner in my life, or hadn't been so angry with others. Don't stay angry with those you should care about. We've seen many people forced to live with regret after angry words, or years of noncommunication due to a ridiculous difference of opinion took place. Is it so very important to be right?

- It isn't about me. It's all about Jesus. There are so many books out there in the world that tell us the five things we can do to get God to hear our prayers;

the seven things we can do to be highly effective Christians; the twelve things we can do to get God to bless us; and on and on. All of those things focus on us. They all put the emphasis on what we can do to get God to do something. They are all works based instead of faith based. It is imperative that we remember Jesus already did it *all*! Everything we need is already paid for and provided. If you need it, it is already accessible. All we have to do is believe in the one who sacrificed Himself for us to provide it and receive what is already available!

- If you want to know what is important to someone, watch where they spend their money, their effort, and their time. I had to take a good hard look at this one after my husband and I married. I was frightened to give. I'd grown up without much, and I felt that if I gave, I would be left without enough to get by. Once we started giving, we discovered you cannot outgive God, and besides, the giving part is so much fun!

Nothing in the world gives us more joy now than to share what we have with others who need. To feed the hungry, put shoes on the feet of little children, dig wells to provide clean water for villages, to give for cancer research, to support wounded warriors; or families in South and Central America, India, and Africa. Something which has become a real joy to us is to give to families at Christmas so they can have presents for their children. We have never felt as alive as when we are able to help others! Try it, you will be amazed. Once you take the focus off yourself and begin doing the things God has put on your heart to do, your spirit will soar!

- You catch more flies with honey than you do with vinegar. This is a good one. I used to argue with people about the Gospel. We are supposed to be at peace, as much as is possible, with people, but I had a problem with people disagreeing with me. It can be different if someone is on the edge of believing, if they just need a little nudge and if a bit of apologetics will be the one thing they needed to hear to trust Jesus, but if they continue to argue, to need more and more proof, and refuse to hear the truth, then it isn't my job to argue with them. I will be kind and share with whoever will listen, but I don't have to defend God. He can take care of Himself!

- We are God's ambassadors. Wherever we go, people are watching. More often than not, if they know you are a Christian, they are looking for ways to trip you up. Many will make up stories and try to cause trouble in your life, to defame you, but we are here to represent God's love and grace everywhere we go. I am an example at all times. I can either be a godly example or an ungodly one. I choose to represent my God by showing His love to others.

- Don't be afraid to be the one who loves the most. In my younger years, I was afraid to love. Everyone I'd ever loved had hurt me so badly I felt I couldn't take that chance. A friend told me I should strive to be the one who loves the least in my relationships, so that I would have all the power. I can assure you it does not work. Having the power isn't all it's cracked up to be. If we are going to love, we must love with our whole heart. We must love with the love of Christ.

- Let it go. Stop worrying. There are many things we can't control, and it doesn't do any good to lie in bed and fret all night. Turn it over to God, because He will be up all night anyway. Pray, get a good night's sleep, and tackle the problem, with God's help, in the morning after you're rested.

- He loves me. I am His beloved and His favored one. I am the righteousness of God in Christ!

- I will continue to love and serve Him even if I never get the things I've asked for. I used to wonder how I would feel if it seemed that God never answered my prayers. I came to the realization that He is for me and always looking out for my best interests, so if I don't have something, then my life must be better off without it. I will trust Him alone.

Don't Give Up
on Your Dreams

Don't talk yourself out of your dreams and goals! God never gives up on the dreams He's placed in your heart. They are a part of His ultimate plan, and He will help you achieve them if you trust Him and believe.

Perhaps circumstances got in your way; maybe you didn't have the resources to fund your ideas; you might have been a late bloomer; perhaps you were raising a family; or even experienced a personal tragedy, which held you back. Take heart, it is never too late to follow your dreams. What follows are a few of the many hundreds of famous individuals who got a later start in life.

Julia Child. Went to cooking school at age thirty-six, began cooking at age forty, and finally started her popular cooking show at age fifty.

Stan Lee (the creator of Spider-Man). Didn't begin drawing until he was forty-three. His partner Jack Kirby developed the Fantastic Four at the age of forty-four.

Sir Alexander Fleming. Discovered penicillin at the age of forty-seven and went on to win a Nobel Prize at the age of sixty-four.

Oscar Swahn. Won two gold medals in the 1908 Olympics at the age of sixty, then won another gold at the 1912 Olympics at age sixty-four, and finally won a silver medal at the 1920 Olympics at age seventy-two.

Ben Franklin. Achieved many things throughout his life, but at age seventy, he signed the Declaration of Independence; at age seventy-seven, he negotiated the Treaty of Paris, and then at age eighty-one, he signed the Constitution of the United States.

Harlan Sanders. Created the most famous chicken brand in the world, Kentucky Fried Chicken, at the age of sixty-six.

Laura Ingalls Wilder. Wrote the *Little House on the Prairie* books; wasn't published until she was sixty-four.

Ronald Regan. Was sixty-nine when he was elected president of the United States.

Mother Teresa. Was sixty-nine when she was awarded the Nobel Peace Prize.

Grandma Moses. Didn't start painting until she was seventy-five years old.

Ray Kroc. Founded McDonald's when he was fifty-two.

Golda Meir. Was seventy when she became the fourth prime minister of Israel.

Nelson Mandela. Became president of South Africa at seventy-four.

Peter Roget. Published Roget's Thesaurus at the age of seventy-three.

Mary Wesley. Had her first novel published at the age of seventy-one.

The list goes on and on! I am sixty-one years old and had already seen my share of rejection letters before the publishing of this book, but if we have faith and never, ever give up, God will see the dreams

He's put in our hearts, which are in line with His will, come to fruition.

For years, I justified my hesitance to follow through with my dreams of being a writer. I felt it was too late for me. I raised my family, completed a career in management, and made the mistake of listening to people who reminded me I wasn't a youngster anymore. After doctors told me I had a terminal illness, I needed something to occupy my time, so I began to write. Between surgeries and treatments, I wrote endlessly, and I discovered I love writing! Ironic how being told you don't have much time left can spur you on to accomplish your dreams. Don't let others talk you out of your dreams, your goals, and your victories. God wants to give you the desires of your heart.

> Delight yourself in the Lord, and He will give you the desires of your heart. Commit your way to the Lord; trust Him, and He will act (Ps. 37:4–5, ESV).

I have a friend who always dreamed of being a chef. She was an excellent cook and knew this was her ultimate heart's desire, but she didn't have a culinary degree and felt she wasn't qualified. She talked about going back to school, but her family told her she was too old to go after her dreams. They told her the culinary industry was for a younger person and that ship had sailed. Whenever I saw an advertisement in the paper for an open chef's position, I'd call her and she would make excuses as to why she wouldn't be able to apply for the job. Finally, a position opened and the restaurant was holding open auditions for the position.

Instead of looking at degrees, they were going to let cooking ability win the day. My friend balked, but I was determined to see her dream fulfilled so I called and made an appointment in her name. She was furious with me at first, but eventually gave in and agreed to show up for her tryout. Auditions were held in the restaurant's kitchen and were being timed, which would be an additional pressure. She'd be expected to make a variety of entrees, an appetizer, and a dessert in a harried environment.

We prayed together, and she prepared her station. Due to her age, fifty-three, her cooking experience and her calm demeanor, she was able to get through all her tasks in a timely and professional manner. She was told she'd be called in for a second interview if the owners were interested and we left. I thought she would still be angry with me, but instead she was exhilarated.

Telling me no matter how this audition played out, she was pleased with how well she'd done and was no longer afraid of pursuing a career in the culinary arts. Dozens of others applied for the same position, so my friend was pretty sure the job would go to someone younger, or with more experience, but when the end of the week came, she was called in for an interview. Her interview went great, and she was hired for the position! She eventually went on to travel for the company and act as a trainer. She is seeing the world and being paid for doing what she loves!

I've known too many people who waited for their dreams, too afraid to pursue them, or too deceived to believe they deserved them. When talking to nursing home residents later in life, I might ask them in a conversation what they did for a living when they were younger, and it makes me very sad to hear, "Oh, I wanted to be a…but I got stuck doing…." The sad epitaph of a derailed dream.

Don't do what some of us have done and put off your dreams. You might feel as I did years ago that you don't want to bother God by asking Him to fulfill your dreams and give you the desires of your heart. "I mean, after all, God must have better things to do than care about my dumb dreams." But remember, God placed those dreams in your heart for a purpose, and He wants to help you achieve them. Believe and receive what He has already provided.

The saddest unfulfilled dream is a dream of being accepted by God, which is never realized. Too many believe they must clean up their act before they can approach a Holy God and ask for forgiveness through Christ. To die before coming to trust Jesus means an eternity of hell. That is not a future God wants for any of us. Come to Him now, imperfect and broken, just the way you are, just as the rest of us have come. Enjoy an eternity of peace and rest, of love and joy with the Father, the living God. Then pray. God loves bold confident prayers—prayers that let Him know you trust Him! Ask for anything your heart desires, and if it lines up with His Word, then wait in positive expectation!

My family and I have waited in positive expectation, trusting Him and believing His promises now for five years. I won't tell you that those years have been easy, but they have been years of miracles, growth, stretching, and learning; and promises fulfilled. God is good ALL the time.

In October I went in for routine scans and when I met with Shari for the results a few days later she admitted to me that she hadn't been looking forward to these scans; in particular because of the spot on my breast bone. But, she was happy to announce that I am clear. Completely clear! There is no more evidence of disease in my left lung, or on my breast bone of the cancer and God has proved once again that He is the Great Physician, and my loving Father!

Follow Me as I Follow Christ

What is the definition of the word *Christian*? The definition is "a person who follows the teachings of Christ." Do I follow Christ? Do I emulate Christ for those who are watching me? Those are questions I ask myself frequently these days. Many believe they are following Christ, or acting in a Christian manner without the proper information. The Bible is God's instruction book for our lives. Everything we will ever need to know about how to treat others, or how to follow Him is written on the pages of that instruction manual.

What a Christian is: If we are following Christ, we are love and will treat others with love. We are kind and compassionate.

> Beloved, let us love one another, for love is from God and whoever loves has been born of God and knows God. Anyone who does not love does not know God, because God is love. (1 John 4:7–8, ESV)

> The Lord is gracious and compassionate, slow to anger and abounding in steadfast love. (Ps. 145:8, ESV)

> When He saw the crowds, He had compassion for them, because they were harassed and helpless, like sheep without a shepherd. (Matt. 9:36, ESV)

If we are Christians, we are wise as serpents and innocent as doves.

> Behold, I am sending you out as sheep in the midst of wolves, so be wise as serpents and innocent as doves (Matt. 10:16, ESV).

If we are Christians, we are giving, and we have a heart for the less fortunate.

> But he desiring to justify himself, said to Jesus, "And who is my neighbor?" Jesus replied, "A man was going down from Jerusalem

to Jericho and he fell among robbers, who stripped him and beat him and departed, leaving him half dead. Now by chance a priest was going down that road, and when he saw him he passed by on the other side. So likewise a Levite, when he came to the place and saw him, passed by on the other side. But a Samaritan, as he journeyed, came to where he was, and when he saw him, he had compassion. He went to him and bound up his wounds, pouring on oil and wine. Then he set him on his own animal and brought him to an inn and took care of him. And the next day he took out two denarius and gave them to the innkeeper, saying, 'Take care of him, and whatever more you spend, I will repay you when I come back.' Which of these three, do you think, proved to be a neighbor to the man who fell among the robbers?" He said, "The one who showed him mercy." And Jesus said to him, "You go and do likewise." (Luke 10:29–37, ESV)

Religion that is pure and undefiled before God, the Father, is this: to visit orphans and widows in their affliction, and to keep oneself unstained from the world. (James 1:27, ESV)

If we are Christians, we will live lives that are healed and whole, and we will do those things which Christ did and more.

> And these signs will accompany those who believe; in my name they will cast out demons; they will speak in new tongues; they will pick up serpents with their hands; and if they drink any deadly poison, it will not hurt them; they will lay their hands on the sick, and they will recover. (Mark 16:17–18, ESV)
>
> Truly, truly, I say to you, whoever believes in me will also do the works that I do; and greater works than these will he do, because I am going to the Father. (John 14:12, ESV)

If we are Christians we are more than conquerors!

> No, in all these things we are more than conquerors through Him who loved us. For I am sure that neither death nor life, nor angels nor rulers, nor things present nor things to come, nor powers, nor height nor depth, nor anything else in all creation, will be able to separate us from the love of God in Christ Jesus our Lord." (Rom. 8:37–39, ESV)

If we are Christians, we are children of the Most High God and joint heirs with Christ!

> For you did not receive the spirit of slavery to fall back into fear, but you have received the spirit of adoption as sons, by whom we cry, Abba! Father! The Spirit Himself bears witness with our spirit that we are children of God, and if children, then heirs—heirs of God and fellow heirs with Christ, provided we suffer with Him in order that we may also be glorified with Him. (Rom. 8:15–17, ESV)

Have you ever met someone who claims to be a Christian, but when you ask them if they have Jesus as their Savior, they tell you what church they attend, or tell you they know who God is? Even the devil knows who God is, but that doesn't mean he is a follower of Christ.

> You believe that God is one; you do well. Even the demons believe—and shudder! (James 2:19, ESV).

Am I a sinner? If I am a human being, I am a sinner. I am not a sinner because I sin. I sin because I am a sinner. We are all born into Adam's sinful nature. In the same vein, I am not righteous because I don't sin. I am righteous because I believe on Christ and therefore gain the gift of righteousness through His sacrifice. Now I need to make a decision as to whether I want to remain a lost sinner or accept a free gift of salvation through Christ.

> But now the righteousness of God has been manifested apart from the law, although the Law and the Prophets bear witness to it—the righteousness of God through faith in Jesus Christ for all who believe. For there is no distinction: for all have sinned and fall short of the glory of God, and are justified by His grace as a gift, through the redemption that is in Christ Jesus, whom God put forward as a propitiation by His blood, to be received by faith. This is to show God's righteousness, because in His divine forbearance He had passed over former sins. It was to show His righteousness at the present time, so that He might be just and the justifier of the one who has faith in Jesus. (Rom. 3:21–26, ESV)

Remember that there is a big difference between being a professing Christian and a possessing Christian. Do you want to know that when you leave this place, you will be in the arms of Jesus? Have you decided to follow Christ? All you must do is admit to Him that you are a sinner, admit that you are helpless to do anything about it on your own and ask Him to save you and to live in you. Once you have done that you are a child of God. Welcome to the family!

FAVORITE SCRIPTURE VERSES

What follows are some of the scripture verses which got me through some very difficult times after my first cancer diagnosis. I have gathered them together for easier access, since I quite frequently read through them for my own edification. I hope that you will spend time reading the Word for yourself and digging out some favorite scriptures, but the following is a good place to start.

"As for you, you meant evil against me, but God meant it for good, to bring it about that many people should be kept alive, as they are today" (Gen. 50:20, ESV).

"The Lord will fight for you, and you have only to be silent" (Exod. 14:14, ESV).

"The Lord is my shepherd; I shall not want" (Ps. 23:1, ESV).

"You prepare a table before me in the presence of my enemies; you anoint my head with oil; my cup overflows. Surely goodness and mercy shall follow me all the days of my life, and I shall dwell in the house of the Lord forever" (Ps. 23:5–6, ESV).

"May the Lord give strength to His people! May the Lord bless His people with peace" (Ps. 29:11, ESV).

"Many are the afflictions of the righteous, but the Lord delivers him out of them all" (Ps. 34:19, ESV).

"God is our refuge and strength, a very present help in trouble" (Ps. 46:1, ESV).

"Blessed be the Lord, who daily bears us up; God is our salvation, and to God, the Lord belong deliverances from death" (Ps. 68:19–20, ESV).

"But I will hope continually and will praise you yet more and more" (Ps. 71:14, ESV).

"For the Lord God is a sun and shield; the Lord bestows favor and honor. No good thing does He withhold from those who walk uprightly" (Ps. 84:11, ESV).

"Because you have made the Lord your dwelling place-the Most High, who is my refuge—no evil shall be allowed to befall you, no plague come near your tent" (Ps. 91:9–10, ESV).

"Bless the Lord, O my soul, and forget not all His benefits, who forgives all your iniquity, who heals all your diseases, who redeems your life from the pit, who crowns you with steadfast love and mercy, who satisfies you with good so that your youth is renewed like the eagle's" (Ps. 103:2–5, ESV).

"Praise the Lord! Oh, give thanks to the Lord, for He is good! For His mercy endures forever" (Ps. 106:1, ESV).

"The Lord will keep you from all evil; He will keep your life" (Ps. 121:7, ESV).

"The wicked flee when no one pursues, but the righteous are bold as a lion" (Prov. 28:1, ESV).

"Fear not, for I am with you; be not dismayed, for I am your God; I will strengthen you, I will help you, I will uphold you with my righteous right hand" (Isa. 41:10, ESV).

"But He was wounded for our transgressions; He was crushed for our iniquities; upon Him was the chastisement that brought us peace, and by His stripes we are healed" (Isa. 53:5, ESV).

"No weapon that is fashioned against you shall succeed, and you shall confute every tongue that rises against you in judgment. This is the heritage of the servants of the Lord and their vindication from me, declares the Lord" (Isa. 54:17, ESV).

"So shall my Word be that goes out from my mouth; it shall not return to me empty, but it shall accomplish that which I purpose, and shall succeed in the thing for which I sent it" (Isa. 55:11, ESV).

"Then the Lord said to me, "You have seen well, for I am watching over my word to perform it" (Jer. 1:12, ESV).

"For I know the plans I have for you, declares the Lord, plans for your welfare and not for evil, to give you a future and a hope. Then you will call upon me and come and pray to me, and I will hear you" (Jer. 29:11–12, ESV).

"Ask, and it will be given to you, seek and you will find, knock and it will be opened to you. For everyone who asks receives, and the one who seeks finds, and to the one who knocks it will be opened" (Matt. 7:7–8, ESV).

"And these signs will accompany those who believe; in my name they will cast out demons; they will speak in new tongues; they will pick up serpents with their hands; and if they drink any deadly poison, it will not hurt them; they will lay their hands on the sick, and they will recover" (Mark 16:17–18, ESV).

"For nothing will be impossible with God" (Luke 1:37, ESV).

"But let him ask in faith, with no doubting, for he who doubts is like a wave of the sea driven and tossed by the wind" (John 1:6, ESV).

"So if the Son sets you free, you will be free indeed" (John 8:36, ESV).

"We know that God does not listen to sinners, but if anyone is a worshipper of God and does His will, He listens to him" (John 9:31, ESV).

"The thief comes only to steal and kill and destroy. I came that they may have life and have it abundantly" (John 10:10, ESV).

"I give them eternal life, and they will never perish, and no one will snatch them out of my hand. My Father, who has given them to me, is greater than all, and no one is able to snatch them out of the Father's hand" (John 10:28–29, ESV).

"Jesus said to her, "I am the resurrection and the life. Whoever believes in me, though he die, yet shall he live" (John 11:25, ESV).

"Whatever you ask in my name, this I will do, that the Father may be glorified in the Son" (John 14:13, ESV).

"These things I have spoken to you, that my joy may be in you, and that your joy may be full" (John 15:11, ESV).

"Until now you have asked nothing in my name. Ask, and you will receive, that your joy may be full" (John 16:24, ESV).

"I have said these things to you, that in me you may have peace. In the world you will have tribulation. But take heart; I have overcome the world" (John 16:33, ESV).

"But you will receive power when the Holy Spirit has come upon you, and you will be my witnesses in

Jerusalem and in all Judea and Samaria, and to the end of the earth" (Acts 1:8, ESV).

"And now I commend you to God and to the Word of His Grace, which is able to build you up and to give you the inheritance among all those who are sanctified" (Acts 20:32, ESV).

"No distrust made him waver concerning the promise of God, but he grew strong in his faith as he gave glory to God fully convinced that God was able to do what He had promised" (Rom. 4:20–21, ESV).

"Therefore, since we have been justified by faith, we have peace with God through our Lord Jesus Christ" (Rom. 5:1, ESV).

"If the Spirit of Him who raised Jesus from the dead dwells in you, He who raised Christ Jesus from the dead will also give life to your mortal bodies through His Spirit who dwells in you" (Rom. 8:11, ESV).

"For you did not receive the spirit of slavery to fall back into fear, but you have received the spirit of adoption as sons, by whom we cry, Abba! Father! The Spirit Himself bears witness with our spirit that we are children of God, and if children, then heirs-heirs of God and fellow heirs with Christ, provided we suffer with Him in order that we may also be glorified with Him" (Rom. 8:15–17, ESV).

"And we know that for those who love God all things work together for good, for those who are called according to His purpose" (Rom. 8:28, ESV).

"What then shall we say to these things? If God is for us, who can be against us?" (Rom. 8:31, ESV).

"No, in all these things we are more than conquerors through Him who loved us. For I am sure that neither death nor life, nor angels nor rulers, nor things present nor things to come, nor powers, nor height nor depth, nor anything else in all creation, will be able to separate us from the love of God in Christ Jesus our Lord" (Rom. 8:37–39, ESV).

"For our sake He made him to be sin who knew no sin, so that in Him we might become the righteousness of God" (2 Cor. 5:21, ESV).

"What agreement has the temple of God with idols? For we are the temple of the living God; as God said, 'I will make my dwelling among them and walk among them, and I will be their God, and they shall be my people'" (2 Cor. 6:16, ESV).

"And God is able to make all Grace abound to you, so that having all sufficiency in all things at all times, you may abound in every good work" (2 Cor. 9:8, ESV).

"I have been crucified with Christ. It is no longer I who live, but Christ who lives in me. And the life I now live in the flesh I live by faith by the son of God, who loved me and gave Himself for me" (Gal. 2:20, ESV).

"For freedom Christ has set us free, stand firm therefore, and do not submit again to a yoke of slavery" (Gal. 5:1, ESV).

"In Him we have redemption through His blood, the forgiveness of our trespasses, according to the riches of His grace" (Eph. 1:7, ESV).

"But God being rich in mercy, because of the great love with which He loved us, even when we were dead in our trespasses, made us alive together with Christ-by grace you have been saved—and raised us up with Him seated us with Him in the heavenly places in Christ Jesus, so that in the coming ages He might show the immeasurable riches of His grace in kindness toward us in Christ Jesus. For by grace you have been saved through faith. And this is not your own doing; it is the gift of God. Not a result of works, so that no one may boast" (Eph. 2:4–9, ESV).

"But now in Christ Jesus you who once were far off have been brought near by the blood of Christ. For He Himself is our peace, who has made us both one and has broken down in His flesh the dividing wall of hostility by abolishing the law of commandments expressed in ordinances, that He might create in Himself one new man in place of the two, so making peace, and might reconcile us both to God in one body through the cross, thereby killing the hostility. And He came and preached peace to you who were far off and peace to those who were near. For through Him we both have access in one Spirit to the Father. So then you are no longer strangers and aliens, but you are fellow Citizens with the saints and members of the household of God, built on the foundation of the apostles and prophets, Christ Jesus Himself being the cornerstone, in whom the whole structure being joined together, grows into a holy temple in the Lord. In Him you also are being built together into a dwelling place for God by the Spirit" (Eph. 2:13–22, ESV).

"Now to Him who is able to do far more abundantly than all that we ask or think, according to the power at work within us, to Him be glory in the church and in Christ Jesus throughout all generations, forever and ever, Amen" (Eph. 3:20–21, ESV).

"For it is God who works in you, both to will and to work for His good pleasure" (Phil. 2:13, ESV).

"Do not be anxious about anything, but in everything by prayer and supplication with thanksgiving let your requests be made known to God. And the peace of God, which surpasses all understanding, will guard your hearts and your minds in Christ Jesus" (Phil. 4:6–7, ESV).

"I can do all things through Christ who strengthens me" (Phil. 4:13, ESV).

"And my God will supply every need of yours according to His riches in glory in Christ Jesus" (Phil. 4:19, ESV).

"For God gave us a sprit not of fear but of power and love and self control" (2 Tim. 1:7, ESV).

"So then, there remains a Sabbath rest for the people of God, for whoever has entered God's rest has also rested from his works as God did from His" (Heb. 4:9–10, ESV).

"Let us hold fast the confession of our hope without wavering, for He who promised is faithful" (Heb. 10:23, ESV).

"Now faith is the assurance of things hoped for, the conviction of things not seen" (Heb. 11:1, ESV).

"And without faith it is impossible to please Him, for whoever would draw near to God must believe that He exists and that He rewards those who seek Him" (Heb. 11:6, ESV).

"So we can confidently say, 'The Lord is my helper; I will not fear; what can man do to me?'" (Heb. 13:6, ESV).

"He Himself bore our sins in His body on the tree, that we might die to sin and live to righteousness. By His wounds you have been healed" (1 Pet. 2:24, ESV).

"For the eyes of the Lord are on the righteous, and His ears are open to their prayer. But the face of the Lord is against those who do evil" (1 Pet. 3:12, ESV).

"Humble yourselves, therefore, under the mighty hand of God so that at the proper time He may exalt you, casting all your anxieties on Him, because He cares for you" (1 Pet. 5:6–7, ESV).

"His divine power has granted to us all things that pertain to life and godliness, through the knowledge of Him, who called us to His own glory and excellence" (2 Pet. 1:3, ESV).

"And this is the promise that He made to us—eternal life" (1 John 2:25, ESV).

"Little children, you are from God and have overcome them, for He who is in you is greater than he who is in the world" (1 John 4:4, ESV).

"By this we know that we abide in Him and He in us, because He has given us of His Spirit. And we have seen and testify that the Father has sent His Son to be the Savior of the world. Whoever confesses that Jesus is the Son of God, God abides in him and he in God. So we have come to know and to believe the love that God has for us. God is love, and whoever abides in love abides in God, and God abides in him. By this is love perfected with us, so that we may have confidence for the Day of Judgment, because as He is so are we in this world. There is no fear in love, but perfect love casts out fear. For fear has to do with punishment, and whoever fears has not been perfected in love. We love because He first loved us. If anyone says 'I love God,' and hates His brother, he is a liar; for he who does not love his brother whom he has seen cannot love God whom he has not seen. And this commandment we have from Him: whoever loves God must also love his brother" (1 John 4:13–21, ESV).

"And this is the confidence that we have toward Him, that if we ask anything according to His will He hears us. And if we know that He hears us in whatever we ask, we know that we have the requests that we have asked of Him" (1 John 5:14–15, ESV).

"And they have conquered him by the blood of the Lamb and by the word of their testimony, for they loved not their lives even unto death" (Rev. 12:11, ESV).

"He will wipe away every tear from their eyes, and death shall be no more, neither shall there be mourning, nor crying, nor pain anymore, for the former things have passed away" (Rev. 21:4, ESV).

CPSIA information can be obtained
at www.ICGtesting.com
Printed in the USA
FFHW01n1744170918

9 781947 143029